CHINOOK: A HISTORY AND DICTIONARY

CHINOOK

A History and Dictionary
Of the Northwest Coast Trade Jargon

THE CENTURIES-OLD TRADE LANGUAGE OF THE INDIANS OF THE PACIFIC.

A HISTORY OF ITS ORIGIN AND ITS ADOPTION AND USE BY THE TRADERS, TRAPPERS, PIONEERS AND EARLY SETTLERS OF THE NORTHWEST COAST.

By

EDWARD HARPER THOMAS

BINFORDS & MORT, *Publishers*

Portland • Oregon • 97242

Chinook: A History and Dictionary

LIBRARY OF CONGRESS CATALOG NUMBER: 79-116971
ISBN: O-8323-0217-1

Printed in the United States of America

SECOND EDITION

CONTENTS

Part One: A History

Part Two: A Dictionary

v

INTRODUCTION

IT IS NOW MORE THAN A HUNDRED years since the first attempt was made to compile a dictionary of the Chinook Jargon, the early trade language of the Pacific Northwest. This Jargon was in use among the natives of the region when the first explorers and maritime traders arrived. Captain John Meares used a Jargon word when he related in his Journal, in 1788, that the exclamation of Nootkan Chief Callicum, on tasting blood, was *cloosh*. *Cloosh* is equivalent to the Jargon word *kloshe* meaning "good."

John Rodgers Jewitt, in his account of his captivity among the Nootkans, 1803-05, as the personal slave of Chief Maquinna, gave what purported to be a Nootkan vocabulary of some eighty words. In it are ten which are found in the Chinook Jargon. Captains Meriwether Lewis and William Clark were spoken to in the Jargon by Chinook Chief Concomly, when they were camped on the north side of the Columbia in the fall of 1805.

At the time the words were recorded they were thought to be from the tribal dialect of the Nootkans on the west coast of Vancouver Island and from that of the Chinooks at the mouth of the Columbia. These three widely separated circumstances furnish the first records of the existence of the as-yet-unsuspected Jargon. Neither Meares nor Lewis and Clark had any inkling that there were two languages in use among these tribes. Jewitt arrived at this conclusion in trying to render a Nootkan war song into English, but he had had no intercourse with any but the Nootkans and could not know that the words he learned and wrote in 1804 or 1805 were being written at the same time into the records of Lewis and Clark at the mouth of the Columbia. Jewitt believed the Nootkans had

vii

two languages, one for poetical expression and the other for every-day use.

By 1811 John Jacob Astor had founded Astoria, and ten years later the Hudson's Bay Company had established itself on the Columbia. In the meantime the explorers and traders had been coming by land. Somewhere and sometime during this period the existence of the Jargon became known. All the Indians talked it to each other and resorted to it in their conversations with the whites. Knowledge of this trade language became a necessary part of the trader's equipment.

The first serious attempt to reduce it to writing was probably that of Blanchet, an early missionary in Oregon. He and his companion, Father Demers, had to instruct numerous tribes of Indians as well as the wives and children of the whites, all of whom spoke the Chinook Jargon. These two missionaries mastered the language quickly and began to preach, using it as their medium of communication. Father Demers composed a vocabulary, used the Jargon for the words of the canticles his people were taught to sing, translated into it all the Christian prayers and used it exclusively in all their services and work of instruction.

Since that time something more than fifty dictionaries and vocabularies have been compiled, printed and used, some of them quite primitive, restricted and crude. George C. Shaw's Dictionary, *The Chinook Jargon and How To Use It* (1909), stands out from all others in its completeness. In compiling his work Mr. Shaw went exhaustively into all the standard authorities, examining every previously published volume pertaining to the Jargon, and every document and unpublished manuscript available as well. His research was careful and painstaking and his dictionary is in all respects authoritative.

The present volume embodies Shaw, and for the first time since his dictionary appeared, attempts to go farther, in that it searches out the origin of the Jargon, goes into the history of this strange tongue from the first recorded words found in the logs and journals of the earliest explorers, and by comparing them finds that the Jargon was in such common use among tribes spread over a wide area as to preclude any but the theory that for centuries it must have been the one great vehicle of communication in prehistoric tribal trading intercourse. This book, therefore, is a narrative history and complete lexicon of the Chinook Jargon.

Knowing the value of Mr. Shaw's work, and the labor it would save in re-examining all the authorities he scrutinized so closely, the author of this book purchased from him his interest in *The Chinook Jargon and How To Use It*, taking from him an assignment of his copyright and recording it with the Register of Copyrights at Washington.

Among other notable compilations, the most authoritative is that of George Gibbs, who spent twelve years on the Northwest Coast in the first half of the past century. After Gibbs, the most important work was done by Horatio Hale. The Jargon was also studied by many authorities including Henry Schoolcraft, Franz Boas, Myron Eells, Charles Tate, Tertius Hibben, James Swan, John Gill, and others.

Around 1875, fully one hundred thousand persons spoke the Jargon. Among all the generations since 1811, or thereabouts, it has been used by upwards of a quarter million persons, to many of whom it was an everyday necessity.

The Jargon was so widely used because—though short on beauty and refinement of detail—it was able to communicate successfully between persons of different tribes, nationalities, and races. It was practical and unpretentious. It absorbed what was useful and discarded the useless.

When the Nootkans paddled down the coast to *makuk*, or trade, the Clatsops and Chinooks added that word to their own vocabulary; and it little mattered how it should be spelled—*makuk* or the later *mahkook*. Theirs was not a written jargon but an oral one—a communal language that was democratic in its make-up. It had to be based on sounds pronounceable by a wide variety of linguistic groups.

As the French-Canadian and English and American traders invaded Indian country, the natives were introduced to an impressive number of new objects, which required names; and new sounds, which they attempted to imitate. However, their imitation often fell far short of the original—which bothered the users of the Jargon not at all.

Some of the most involved adaptations were from the French. French Jargon words often bore little likeness to the original French spelling, when recorded by later compilers of Jargon dictionaries. An interesting example is the French word for mother—*mere*—which like other French words clung to its article *la* (the), when taken over by the Indians. In the Jargon, *la mere* lost the *r* sound because of the difficulty they had pronouncing it; so, we find the word mother written *lamai, lummieh, lumnei*, and so forth. Further, in the Jargon, *lamai* came to mean "old woman." They had their Nootkan word *klootchman* (from the Nootkan *klootsma*) for the words woman, wife, or female; and a mother was definitely an older woman, a matron. Note, though, that in the Jargon, "man" is simply *man* and "old man" is *oleman*, only slightly changed from the English. Because the Indian male did the trading and the more important "communicating," presumably in early times he needed no particular designation. It was an oral language and he was the speaker.

Generally, when the French word was feminine gender, as *la mere*, the *la* became an integral part of the later recorded form, the same being true of the masculine form *le* (the). For example, in the Jargon, it was *le pan* (bread), *le sak* (sack or bag), or *le seezo* (scissors). The Chinook-English Dictionary contains a number of words starting with *la* and *le*, with hyphens showing the close relationship: *le-pan, le-sak,* and *le-seezo.* In the English-Chinook Dictionary these forms are further tightened to: *lepan, lesak,* and *le-seezo,* or sometimes just plain *sezo.*

An occasional word in the Jargon developed from more than one language, when it was necessary to combine several words to achieve the total meaning. If you look up the word "grog" in the English-Chinook Dictionary, you will find an awkward but intriguing combination of letters forming the Chinook word *lumpechuck* (rum and water, or grog). Broken down into its origin, *lumpechuck* becomes quite reasonable. The Indian had difficulty with his *r*'s, as in *la mere*. Thus, *lum* came from rum; *pe* (and) from *puis* ("then" in French, but "and" in the Jargon); and *chuck* (water) from the Nootkan *chauk*. Such is the derivation of *lumpechuck*, that famous concoction of rum and water, better known in the Queen's Navy as "grog" or "diluted spirits."

Another example of how the face of a word often changed when absorbed into the Jargon is the word for "helm," or steering apparatus of a ship. A part of this apparatus is the rudder—a new word brought by invaders of the Northwest, who came by sea as well as by land. Look up "helm" in the English-Chinook Dictionary, and here also you will find an odd combination of letters—*ludda*. Again the native had trouble with his *r*'s, and "rudder" began and ended with the troublesome sound. So, "rudder" became *ludda* and referred to the entire steering apparatus.

The Chinook Jargon has given, though, as well as taken. From the Nootkans came *tyee* (chief), from the Salish came *skookum* (strong), and from the French *siwash* (a native rendition of the French *sauvage*, meaning savage or aborigine). In good use in the English language today are *tyee*, *skookum*, and *siwash*, with the same meanings.

In view of the service the Jargon rendered to traders, trappers, Indians, and pioneer settlers, and the fascinating insight this medley of languages gives to a vanished time and culture, it has seemed to the publishers that both the Chinook Jargon and its history are worthy of preservation in a form that will make for permanency. This has been the purpose of the present book.

CHIEF MAQUINNA OF THE NOOTKANS

From 1803-1805, while a personal slave of Chief Maquinna, John Rodgers Jewitt recorded what purported to be a Nootkan vocabulary of some eighty words, a number of which found their way into the Chinook Jargon.

Commerce between the Nootkans and Chinooks required some vehicle of communication. The Nootkans learned some of the simpler and easier words of the Chinook Dialect, and the Chinooks picked up a bit of Nootkan. This interchange of a very few words capable of conveying the simpler ideas of barter and exchange became the nucleus of the Jargon.

Part One: A HISTORY

1. LONG EXISTENCE OF THE NORTHWEST TRIBES

AMONG THE NATIVE RACES OF NORTH AMERICA
the most interesting in many ways were those who originally
occupied the so-called Northwest Coast, the region that lay between
the Rocky Mountains and the Pacific Ocean as far south as the
Klamath country in Oregon and as far north as the long panhandle
of southeastern Alaska.

Their first contact with whites may date back to Drake and Juan
de Fuca. We know that Cook, Meares, Barclay, Vancouver, Fidalgo,
Eliza and other early explorers were among them. But it was not
until the publication of the Journal of Lewis and Clark and the
Narrative of John R. Jewitt that these races and their customs, char-
acteristics and tribal distinctions were given so much as trifling
notice. There were two chieftains mentioned in those early books
whose names, from that time, became interwoven with the history
of the region—Concomly of the Chinooks at the mouth of the Columbia River and Maquinna, *Tyee* of the Nootkans, living on the west
coast of Vancouver Island. Aboriginal history begins with their
names. All that lies back of them is Mystery.

In speculating on the origin of the American aboriginal races we
may weigh probability and possibility and reach approximate conclusions but we will never be able to prove these conclusions to our
own satisfaction.

Among their records are remains of picture writing. Some of the
notations in use evidently had many arbitrary characters, but, with

1

no known key and no way provided to mark the distinction between a figure and a symbol, these remains and relics have become "mute epitaphs of a vanishing race." Lacking a key, these signs, symbols and mysterious fragments of a crude and barbaric record offer little help as a means of studying the origin, history, migrations, social structure, and possible tribal relations of the native American races.

There is no starting point, aside from generic racial likenesses, apparently traceable from the Asiatic continent to the American, and broad similarities in myths and traditions held in common. Nor is there any charted course, in the absence of a record, to follow other than these few surviving relics and crudely drawn picture characters that have been mentioned. These, because of their unrelatedness, bewilder rather than aid in the pursuit of any scientifically conclusive research.

Two theories about these aboriginal tribes, however, seem certain: they were here for a very long time and theirs was a sparse population.

Apparently there was a long period between the Cliff Dwellers and the savages known to the first explorers of the Southwest. It seems equally true that the Mound Builders and the Indians of La Salle's day were far from contemporaneous.

There are shell deposits on the Maine coast and shell dikes on Puget Sound—one at Birch Bay, particularly—which can be nothing less than accumulations or slow accretions of a more or less stable population over a long period of time.

These races subsisted mainly upon the chase. The hunters and fishers were the providers of the family and tribal larders. An adequate game supply could co-exist, century after century, only with a sparse population.

The 1910 census shows 400,000 people of native Indian and mixed Indian blood—*Indian* descent—on all the American continent north of Mexico, Alaska and the Eskimo fringe of the Arctic shores included. As only a comparatively few of all the tribes are extinct, this bears out the sparsely populated theory. James Mooney, a

United States government expert, estimated the 1492 population of the continent, exclusive of Mexico, at 1,115,000.

A sparse population, here for a relatively short time, could not have left the shell mounds and dikes, the flint and stone arms and tools, the copper implements, the earth mounds of the Ohio valley, the cliff dwellings and other relics, distributed as they were over the wide and unrelated areas on which they have been found. These evidences in the aggregate preclude any but the theory of long-time occupation.

2. FIXED LINGUAL SIMILARITIES

THE THEORY OF COMMON ORIGIN IS SUPPORTED by certain fixed similarities found in the languages spoken by all the native tribes, the most pronounced of which is that of idiom and the order of words in sentence building. The theory is also supported by the narrative style in the literal translations of myths and texts.

Daniel G. Brinton comments on this theory in his *Myths of the New World* (1868):

> The spoken and written language of a nation reveals to us its prevailing, and to a certain degree its unavoidable mode of thought. Here the red race offers a notable phenomenon. Scarcely any other trait, physical or mental, binds together its scattered clans so unmistakably as that of language. From the Frozen Ocean to the Land of Fire, with few exceptions, the native dialects, though varying endlessly in words, are alike in certain peculiarities of construction, certain morphological features, rarely found elsewhere on the globe, and nowhere else with such persistence.
>
> So foreign are these traits to the grammar of the Aryan

tongues that it is not easy to explain them in a few sentences. They depend on a peculiarly complex method of presenting the relations of the idea in the word. This construction has been called by some philologists *polysynthesis;* but it is better to retain for its chief characteristic the term originally applied to it by Wilhelm von Humboldt, *incorporation.*

What it is will best appear by comparison. Every grammatical sentence conveys one idea with its modifications and relations. Now a Chinese would express these latter by unconnected syllables, the precise bearing of which could only be guessed by their position; a Greek or a German would use independent words, indicating their relations by terminations meaningless in themselves; a Finn would add syllable after syllable to the end of the principal word, each modifying the main idea; an Englishman would gain the same end chiefly by the use of particles and by position.

Very different from all these is the spirit of an incorporative language. It seeks to unite in the most intimate manner all relations and modifications with the leading idea, to merge one in the other by altering the forms of the words themselves and welding them together, to express the whole in one word, and to banish any conception except as it arises in relation to others. Thus in many American tongues there is, in fact, no word for father, mother, brother, but only for my, your, his father, etc. This has advantages and defects. It offers marvelous facilities for defining the perceptions of the senses with accuracy, but it regards everything in the concrete. It is unfriendly to the nobler labors of the mind, to abstraction and generalization.

In the numberless changes of these languages, their bewildering flexibility, their variable forms, and their rapid alterations, they seem to betray a lack of individuality, and to resemble the vague and tumultuous history of the tribes who employ them. They exhibit at times a strange laxity. It is nothing uncommon for the two sexes to use different names for the same object, and for nobles and vulgar, priests and people, the old and the young, nay, even the married and single, to observe what seems to the European ear quite different modes of expression. Their phonetics are fluctuating, the consonantal sounds often alternating between several which in our tongue are clearly defined.

Families and whole villages suddenly drop words and manufacture others in their places out of mere caprice and superstition, and a few years' separation suffices to produce a marked dialectic difference; though it is everywhere true that the basic radicals of each stock and the main outlines of its grammatical forms reveal a surprising tenacity in the midst of these surface changes. Vocabularies collected by the earliest navigators are easily recognized from existing tongues and the widest wanderings of vagrant bands can be traced by the continued relationship of their dialects to the parent stem.

The validity of these conclusions is shown by the ease with which such ethnologists as Boas have gone from tribe to tribe, mastered their dialects and collected their myths and traditions. Much of the work of Boas was done among tribes remote from each other, widely separated territorially, like the Chinooks and the Tsimshians, who had lived each in its own locality always and whose linguistic differences had centuries since become fixed forms of language.

Verne F. Ray is another who supports the theory that—contrary to popular belief—the Chinook Jargon is of pre-white origin. He observes, in "The Historical Position of the Lower Chinook in the Native Culture of the Northwest" (*Pacific Northwest Quarterly*, Vol. 28, No. 4):

"Aboriginally the mouth of the Columbia River, on both the Washington and Oregon sides, was occupied by natives of the Chinookan linguistic stock. Those residing on the Oregon side were known as the Clatsop, those on the Washington side, the Chinook. The latter extended up the Washington coast as far as the northern shore of Willapa Bay, formerly known as Shoalwater Bay. Adjoining the Chinook and Clatsop in the river valley on the east were the Cathlamet, also Chinookan in speech. These three groups occupied a signally important position in the cultural setting of the Northwest, for within their territory four great streams of travel fused.

"Sea-going canoes from British Columbia and even Alaska met vessels from the southern Oregon coast, while cruder dugouts carrying traders from the Plateau east of the Cascades reached this great commercial center via the Columbia waterway. The fourth route, least important, led overland through the Cascade passes from the interior of southern Washington. The development of the well-known *lingua franca,* Chinook jargon, centered here. This jargon is demonstrably of pre-white origin, contrary to popular belief. It was presumably a response to the demands of native commerce in which speakers of highly divergent languages participated. . . ."

Conditions in primitive days preclude the possibility of any social intercourse except occasional trading, for most of the time they were at war because of long-standing, hereditary enmity. Indians of the woods did not understand the ways of Indians of the prairies, nor did Indians of the mountains understand the ways of the Indians of the sea shores who lived on fish and traveled by canoe. Yet there is the persistence of their particular mode of thought, peculiarities of construction, and the morphological features, mentioned by Brinton, which run through all their dialects and languages.

How striking this is may be seen by even a casual study of the literal interpretations of their tribal myths, whether Chinook or Haida, when rendered into parallel English. There is an actual monotony in the similarity, in the order of words, in the construction of their sentences, and particularly in the imagery and idiom so recognizably Indian.

It seems almost inevitable that there should have existed among them some common ways of intercommunication. Their picture symbols was one. Another was the sign language, by means of which Indians freely communicated with each other though belonging to tribes whose dialects had not one word in common. It is perhaps true that knowledge of the sign language and at one time of the picture symbols, was part of every Indian's education, as much so, no doubt, as his acquired knowledge of the habits of the animals, birds and fishes upon which he subsisted.

But there was still another common medium of communication—the trade language. Over many wide areas the Indians held commerce with each other in the days before civilization found this continent. They traded skins for meat, roots for fish, arrowheads for canoes, the ornaments of one region for the ornaments of another, stone implements for pottery, copper for blankets, baskets for wool, grass or tanned-skin clothes or slaves for shell money.

One of the necessities of such prehistoric activities, when there were only Indians to trade with other Indians, through the centuries before Columbus, was some flexible, easily acquired language which all could learn and use.

3. TRADE LANGUAGES

THERE WERE SEVERAL SUCH JARGONS. One of these (the Mobilian, it is called, though it no longer exists) was in use for centuries; then it fell into disuse and after a time was entirely lost. No one thought of preserving it, even as a philological curiosity. It gave its last expiring gasp more than three-quarters of a century ago.

Mobilian was the trade language of the great curve of the Gulf Coast around which Louisiana, Mississippi, Alabama and Florida are grouped. This Jargon was used first by the aboriginal Americans in their own commerce with each other and then by the Indians and the freebooters, and fortune hunters who came among them in the early European invasion of the region.

By a strange coincidence, at the opposite, the Northwest corner of the United States, another language or Jargon, born of the necessities of the native traders, came into existence and was in use for unknown centuries. It is still occasionally spoken, though no longer for purely trading purposes. It has survived as an interesting relic of the vanishing race and has, to some extent, been incorporated in the history, romance and literature of the Northwest.

The early whites in the Mobile region coveted the territory of the native inhabitants, cared little for their trade—as there was neither gold nor furs to be had—cared less for the Indians and nothing at all for their languages. It was inevitable that these unfortunate native races and their dialects, including this trade Jargon, should have found a common grave. All the white settlers wanted of the Gulf natives was their lands. These they got. Everything else was consigned to oblivion.

A different situation existed in the far Northwest. Here the first contact between the natives and the whites was with explorers and traders. Exploration discovered a wealth of furs. Ships from all countries came to trade in the world's greatest fur marts. These were followed by Astor, the great North West Company, the autocratic and powerful Hudson's Bay Company and hundreds of lesser traders. The Indians were needed. They were the producers of the vast wealth gathered by these great concerns and their independent competitors. On the one hand were thousands of native hunters skilled in the pursuit of the millions of fur-bearing creatures of the woods, streams and tidal waters of this then uncharted region. On the other, were men of Scotland, England, Russia, of the original states and colonies and of the French provinces of Canada. The Indians held the key to all this fur wealth. The whites brought the gewgaws, baubles and implements of civilization to tempt and delight them. This was primitive trade, but it was lucrative trade. The longer the barrel of the musket, the more the canny trader got for it, for it was the rule to pile the furs to be exchanged until their height equaled the length of the coveted gun.

Settlement would have spoiled all this. The fur traders and companies guarded the region jealously against all invasion. Pioneers were not wanted, so the settler was kept out of the country, held back from occupancy of the land, just as long as the traders and

Hudson's Bay factors could maintain their supremacy. The fur companies ruled the region and held it intact for half a century, and then shared it grudgingly with the ever-encroaching pioneer for another third of a century after that.

Astor founded Astoria. The North West Company took it away from him. The Hudson's Bay Company absorbed the North West Company—and later established its principal factory at Fort Vancouver. In a few years the invasion of Oregon began. The Company removed to Nisqually but the restless tide of pioneering immigration came over the Cowlitz trail to Puget Sound and in a few years more crowded the great fur company too close for comfort. It moved again and established the city of Victoria on Vancouver Island. Then gold was discovered on the Fraser. The autocratic rule of the Hudson's Bay Company was broken forever.

At first the only trappers were Indians. They supplied all the furs that went either to the freebooters of the sea or the traders who came overland from the already depleted regions of Canada and our own northern tier of states—territories, then. The Indians were necessary aids and allies to both sea and land traders. Furs were the one resource of the country.

Drake, Juan de Fuca, Cook, Meares, Barclay, Vancouver and all their tribe were explorers and not traders. They came and they went away, but their journals do not record that they were interested in the native either as a type or as a race, in his languages or his customs, except that, perhaps, of cannibalism. Several make mention of this practice, but none of them was aware that the cannibalism referred to was more of a rite than the indulgence of a depraved appetite. All of these explorers were looking for a certain fabled strait which was to lead them by some easy northern way from the Pacific to the Atlantic.

But some of them brought back furs and all of them, no doubt, told their friends and kindred of the fur wealth of the Pacific Northwest. The Russians were already in possession of an immensely profitable trade in the region now known as Alaska. Traders followed in the wake of explorers and came into direct and immediate contact with the native races.

One of the first things the traders learned regarding these tribes was that, while many differing dialects were spoken, there was a second language they all talked, a language of limited vocabulary but quite capable of furnishing an adequate vehicle for trading purposes. Almost the first recorded words of this common language are found in the Journal of the Lewis and Clark expedition. These explorers were in the territory of the Lower Chinooks at the time—the mouth of the Columbia—so this trade language or Jargon got the name of Chinook —Tschinuk, it was spelled at first. The word degenerated into Chinook, just as Tschehalis became Chehalis—and Chinook it is today.

Because it is purely a trade language, the origin of which is unknown, some have advanced the theory that it was an invention of the Hudson's Bay Company. There is evidence, however, that it was in use long before the Hudson's Bay Company appeared on the scene.

The Chinook or Tschinuk tribe—we will from now on use only the later spelling for the tribe and the word will be Chinook—had its own dialect, which differed materially from the dialects of even the nearest neighboring Indians, the Cathlamets or Chehalis, and which bore no resemblance whatever to the dialects of such remoter tribes as the Nootkans, Makahs and Quillayutes—but all spoke this Jargon.

4. THE JARGON BEFORE THE TRADING POST

It must be remembered that all this was taking place—including the voluminous record of Jewett and the meager one of Lewis and Clark, as far as the Jargon was concerned—before the Hudson's Bay Company, Astor, or the North West Fur Company had established posts on the Pacific. It was even before they had sent their scouts, traders or factors into the territory. It was not until April 12, 1811, six years after Lewis and Clark's visit and Jewitt's release from captivity, that Astor planted his American Fur Company near the mouth of the Columbia and founded the present city of Astoria, Oregon. It was in this same year that Astor bought out the Mackinaw Company, rival of the North West Fur Company, and merged it with his own American Fur Company.

The North West Company established its headquarters at Fort William, on Lake Superior, in 1805, and had not as yet penetrated west of the headwaters of the Mississippi.

Though Mackenzie, a partner of the North West Company, had crossed the Rocky Mountains and had reached the Pacific as early as July, 1793, coming out at the mouth of the Bellacoola in British Columbia, no posts were established by any company for some years thereafter. Simon Fraser, John Stuart and David Thompson all came later, traveling in part the trail of Mackenzie, but reaching the Pacific at points much farther south. The men of the North West Company had come as far west and south as Fort Okanogan by the time Astor's expedition reached the mouth of the Columbia. Hearing of possible rivalry, the Northwesters prepared to contest occupancy of this territory, and sent an expedition to the new post at Astoria. In October, 1813, Astoria passed into the possession of the North West Company. Not until then did this concern reach the sea. In 1821 they sold out to the Hudson's Bay Company, which prior to that time had no post on the western ocean; but from that date until driven away by encroaching settlement, the Hudson's Bay people ruled the entire region.

Up to Astor's time the fur trade was entirely one of maritime activity. Between 1811 and 1821 it was taken over and absorbed by men who would dwell among the Indians, marry their women, raise halfbreed families and live with the natives on intimate enough relations to affect their customs, languages and habits of thought.

This seems to establish as a fact that the Jargon was in use among the natives as a trading language long before the trader and trapper arrived on the scene, and that contact with the whites enlarged and enriched it by the addition of many words of French and English derivation.

With the coming of the white man, making known to the Indian the weapons, the luxuries and the vices of civilization, came the need of extending the Chinook to cover new conditions. He could not say "carbine" or "fire" so the words became "calipeen" and "piah." The Canadians called the hand "la main," and the Indian came at last to use nearly the same sound. Thus English and French words were grafted upon the Chinook Jargon.

5. A PREHISTORIC SLAVE TRADE

The Chinooks of the Lower Columbia were one of the most powerful tribes on the Pacific Northwest Coast and by virtue of numbers and warlike qualities held sway over much of the region. They were surrounded by such immediate and lesser tribes as the Clatsops, Cathlamets, Wahkiakums, Chehalis and numerous others extending far up the river to the Klickitats, Nez Perces and Walla Wallas.

Among the tribes along all this coast and far into the interior, slavery was an established and time-honored institution. Taking and selling slaves was a commercial pursuit. The Chinooks dignified it by making it the one great business in which they engaged. They were the profiteers in this particular trade. They made raids upon their neighbors, conquered tribes and villages and sold the victims to other warlike masters living in the wildernesses to the north and northwest.

The Nootkans were among the Chinooks' best customers. That was because they had a monopoly on the shell money supply. In certain comparatively shallow waters of their tribal territory, on submerged shelves and banks known to them and controlled by them, certain small but beautiful shells were found. The supply was limited, which added to their value. The method of fishing for them was one known in those early times only to the Nootkans and favored related tribes. The wealth of the Nootkans lay in these shells. They were the money of all the tribes. The Nootkans coveted slaves and used them for all the labor of the villages, fisheries and camps. The Chinooks could furnish an unfailing supply of slaves. Both these tribes grew rich exchanging shell money and slaves. The Nootkans resold the men and women bought from the Chinooks. It is said that often a slave lost his identity completely and finally had no recollection of his former home or people.

This business required some vehicle of communication. The Nootkans learned some of the simpler and easier words of the Chinook dialect, and the Chinooks picked up a bit of Nootkan.

This interchange of a very few words capable of conveying the simpler ideas of barter and exchange became the nucleus of the Jargon. It was gradually added to by the acquisition of easy Salish and Kwakiutl expressions. A Cathlamet word is broadly Chinook, as the Cathlamets are a Lower Columbia people and rather closely related tribally to the Chinooks. Any Chehalis word is Salish, as the Chehalis belong to that family. The Makahs are entirely surrounded by Salish stock, but are an isolated group of Nootkans, separated from the parent tribe by the straits of Juan de Fuca. A Bellabella word is Kwakiutl, since the Bellabellas are an important tribe of the Kwakiutl family, as are the Heiltsuq and Nimpkish. The Nootkans live on the west coast of Vancouver Island and the Kwakiutl on the east coast and the contiguous mainland of British Columbia.

All of these tribes traded among themselves, using this trade language for the purposes of their commerce. Consequently there are words of all these tribal dialects and family stock tongues to be found in the Jargon.

The theory of this work is that the Jargon had its beginning in the trade necessities of the prehistoric, centuries-old slave and shell money commerce carried on primarily between the Lower Chinooks and the equally powerful, intelligent and enterprising Nootkans; that it slowly developed by accretion in their increasing contact with other Indian nations, taking a word here and a word there from the dialects of other tribes; and that it was finally used by all of the Indians of the Northwest Coast in their commercial relations.

The vocabulary was very limited then, and still is; but the words were flexible and capable of conveying many meanings, depending for that upon emphasis, stress, tone of voice and gesture.

After the traders came, in the early years of the last century, words of French and English origin were added and the Jargon grew into a trade language, comprehensive enough for all purposes of intercourse between all the tribes and all the whites within the territory extending from what is now southern Oregon to southeastern Alaska and from the shores of the Pacific east to the Rocky Mountains. It finally developed into its present-day form.

At one time the Chinook Jargon was spoken by approximately a hundred thousand persons, Indians and whites and mixed bloods. Nearly all of the early settlers of Oregon, Washington and British Columbia, miners, loggers and traders, too, spoke it as fluently and as constantly as the Indians, finding it indispensable because of their intimate and close relations with the natives. The Jargon probably reached its maximum popularity and usefulness in the seventies and then began to go into decline. With the advent of the transcontinental railroads and the consequent inrush of an immigration that wholly submerged the native population, it fell into disuse.

The following material on the Chinooks, Clatsops, and Multnomahs was adapted from John Kaye Gill (1851-1929), an authority on the Jargon.

6. CHINOOKS, CLATSOPS AND COAST TRIBES

The Indians of the Columbia west of Celilo were lighter in color than those of the Missouri and Upper Columbia; also a little under the size of the plains people. They were not as active nor so robust as the eastern tribes, nor so able to endure hard labor and exposure. The men were well made, broad and heavy shouldered from the constant use of the paddle. The women rather inclined to corpulence, and both sexes were bow-legged from sitting in canoes. They were rather peaceably disposed and fairly honest in their dealings with each other, but over-tempted by the strange treasures of the white man and inclined to steal from them.

Among some bands, especially those of the lower Columbia, heads were flattened in infancy, apparently with no harmful effects for the child later on. The dress of the men was a single robe of skins, not covering more than half the body from neck to knee. Most of the robes thus worn by men, and sometimes by women, were made from the skins of the big ground squirrel. Finer skins were also worn, the beaver and the priceless sea otter among them. Neither men nor women wore leggings or moccasins. The women wore skirts of long fringe twisted or braided from the inner bark of the cedar, a beautiful, silky, strong fibre—and sometimes a cape of the same, fastened about their necks, and sometimes a cape or robe of skins. In rainy weather both sexes wore hats or caps woven of grass and fine root-threads.

Their houses were built from planks, which they split with wedges and axes of stone, horn and hardwood. The houses usually contained several families, separated by partitions of woven mats of rushes, which were also hung along the walls and spread on the bank of earth which was left along the sides of the house and upon which they sat and slept. The central part of the house was lower than the sides, and in this the fire was made, and cooking and other indoor work performed. A hole in the roof let out some of the smoke, but they usually had fish hanging from poles overhead, so that they made their smoky houses serve in curing their food. They sometimes built beds of saplings, in bunk fashion, along the sides of their houses.

The women made many mats of rushes and grass, which were brought out when "company" came, and spread for guests to sit or sleep upon.

Camas bread, brick-like cakes of pressed and dried salal berries, dried huckleberries, fern and flag roots, and above all wappatoes, were stored in their houses. Jerked venison in strips and dried and smoked salmon were hung from rafters. Smelt and herring were dried or smoked for winter food, and an important item of the coast tribes' diet was whale and seal oil.

They made wide shelves along their house walls from floor to roof, on which were stored the furs, mats, camas bread, baskets and household stuff.

The Clatsops were Chinooks, and once numerous from Tillamook Head (which separated them from the "Killamux") to the Columbia. These dwindled to a handful many years ago. The Chinooks of the north shore of the Columbia, from Cape Disappointment to Gray's Bay, had their principal village in the days of the Astor enterprise on the west side of Scarborough Hill, near where the modern village of Chinook now is. They had also an "upper village" at Point Ellice and another farther up the Chinook River.

7. MULTNOMAHS AND THEIR NEIGHBORS

The Multnomahs were of the Chinook family. The Tillamooks reported that eighteen tribes lived beyond them to the southeast, all speaking the Tillamook tongue. Farther away in the same direction, they said, were six tribes of a different nation.

Lewis and Clark speak of the tribes along the river from the Willamette to the sea, whose habits, appearance, dress and language were like those of the Chinooks and Clatsops. The latter were a tribe of the Chinooks. The Claxtars, of the Clatskanie Valley, the Cowlitz and the Klickitats were intruders in the lower river country. Doctor Coues says the Claxtars were "a vagrant Athapascan tribe," and were therefore a vast distance from their home people.

A little below the mouth of the Willamette, on the northeast shore of Sauvies (Wappato) Island, was a large village of the Multnomah tribe. A little above this village on the Willamette was a Klickitat town. These Klickitats had driven the Multnomahs from that part of the island in a battle. The Multnomahs occupied the southern and western parts of this large island, and also the Scappoose plain and lowlands. Old Charley Mackay, who knew the lower river and its people from 1800 onward, said the Multnomahs had a large town on the Scappoose Bay near Warren and another near Woodland on the lowlands of Lewis River. The Multnomahs were of Chinook stock.

The Multnomahs were especially fortunate in their surroundings, occupying the lowlands of the Willamette, the greater part of fertile Sauvies Island, the lovely slopes and prairies of the Scappoose country—with the broad bays and inlets reaching inland from the Columbia—and their own river, the Multnomah, now Multnomah Channel.

They had no horses, but plenty of canoes. Horses were used scarcely anywhere on the Columbia shores from The Dalles west. In the lakes of Sauvies Island grew wappatoes, the best food of the western tribes. This plant looks like the calla lily, and grows in rich, muddy soil, usually under two feet of water or even more. The squaws gathered the roots by wading out into the lakes, pushing a small canoe, or paddling out in it and going overboard when they reached the wappato patch. They worked the roots loose from the mud with their toes. The roots then rose to the surface and were thrown into the canoe when the woman was ready to go back to her home. Great flocks of waterfowl fed in these lakes, the wappato being also their favorite food. The large white swan was the wappato digger, long-necked and powerful, and when he raised his head to look for the roots he had sent up, the ducks had often devoured them.

The weapons of hunters and warriors were the flint-tipped lance, bow and arrows, and a mace. The fisherman used a pronged spear, or a long lance with a detachable point of horn such as may still be seen in use among Indians spearing salmon on the Columbia. They wove nets of all kinds—for taking anything from smelt to salmon—from strong fibrous roots, and caught large seafish with curious hooks of bone or ivory. Trout, squawfish and sculpin were caught in great numbers by baits tied to the end of a line, and when a fisherman felt a bite he snatched the fish so quickly that he had it in the canoe before it could let go. The clams of the seashore were a constant supply of food, and their shells were used as spoons or saucers for broth.

All of these tribes were familiar with the Chinook Jargon.

8. EXPLORERS UNAWARE OF JARGON'S EXISTENCE

PRIOR TO 1800 THERE WAS HARDLY ANY REFERence to the Jargon, and then it was not identified as such. Meares gives an account of a chief who hurt his leg and sucking the blood from the wound said, *"Cloosh!" Kloshe* in the Jargon means "good." The word is Nootkan; and Callicum, the Indian who used it, was a Nootkan, a chief but little inferior in rank and authority to Maquinna, the *Tyee* of all the Nootkans. *Tyee* is Nootkan, meaning "great chief." Jewitt frequently uses the word in his narrative.

Jewitt was among the Nootkans as the personal slave of the Tyee or chief, Maquinna, from March, 1803, to July, 1805, one of two survivors of a crew this tribe had massacred in revenge for indignities put upon the chief by the captain of the ship.

Jewitt was rescued by Capt. Samuel Hill, of the brig *Lydia*, of Boston in July, 1806. The *Lydia* sailed on a trading voyage along the coast north of Nootka for several months, and in November, 1806, entered the Columbia. About ten miles up the river—probably at Knappton, near the site of the Point Ellice village of the Chinooks—the vessel traded for furs. Jewitt saw medals among these Indians which had been given by Lewis and Clark in the Spring of 1806.

Lewis and Clark spent the winter of 1805 and 1806 among the Chinooks at the mouth of the Columbia, several hundred miles south and east of Nootka Sound. *Wik* was given by Jewitt as a supposed Nootkan word meaning "no," "not," while Lewis and Clark recorded in their Journal that Concomly said to them, *"Waket commatux"*—

do not understand—when they tried to converse with him. The *wik* of Nootka thus was the *waket* of Concomly, and the *wake* of the Jargon as it is spoken today. Concomly's *commatux* (*kumtux* in the Jargon) was *kummetak* in Nootkan and *kemitak* among the Clayoquots, neighbors of the Nootkans.

Neither the story of Jewitt nor the Journal of Lewis and Clark gives any evidence that the writers of these two contemporaneous accounts of experiences among the Nootkans and Chinooks regarded the words they quoted as other than words of the dialects of these two widely separated and dissimilar tribes, three degrees of latitude and two degrees of longitude apart, and unknown to each other.

Jewitt had an inkling of it; at least of the use of two separate tongues among these people, but reached a wrong conclusion. This is found in a footnote and an appendix to his narrative (Ithaca edition) in which he prints a "War Song of the Nootkan Tribe." In this song occurs the expression *"Ie-yee ma hi-chill,"* which he says means "Ye do not know." But he adds, "This appears to be a poetical mode of expression, the common one for 'you do not know' being *wik-kuma-tush.*" Then he observes, "From this it would seem that *they have two languages,* one for their songs and one for common use."

"You do not know," in the Jargon as it was spoken from 1820 or 1830 on and as it is spoken today, is *"Mika wake kumtux,"* *mika* meaning you.

Jewitt almost discovered the truth. The Nootkans, and all the other northwest tribes, did have two languages; each had its own dialect, and all had the common trade Jargon. The Nootkan tribal songs were in Nootkan, but communication with outsiders was carried on through the polyglot tongue built up by their commerce with each other. Jewitt, of course, was an outsider, a remote foreigner, and these Indians undoubtedly talked to him in mixed Jargon and Nootkan. The Chinooks, from long habit, used the same method when they tried to hold conversation with the men of the Lewis and Clark expedition.

Jewitt left a very limited vocabulary which he calls "a list of words in the Nootkan language the most in use." In it are 87 words, and among these are ten easily recognizable as either belonging to the Jargon or as words in the Nootkan tongue from which the Jargon grew in part. In addition to these ten he makes frequent use of the word *tyee*, which came from the Nootkan into the Jargon and which means "chief" in each instance.

9. JARGON WORDS IN JEWITT'S VOCABULARY

There are two Jargon words used by Jewitt in the Narrative which are not found in his vocabulary. These are *tyee*, referred to before, and *pechak*. *Pechak* is a Nittinat word, and the Nittinats are Nootkan Indians. *Pechak* means bad. Maquinna used the word when he returned the broken musket to Captain Salter of the *Boston; peshak* is the Jargon for bad, but so is *mesachie*. The latter is from the Chinook dialect, and is more commonly used on Puget Sound and the Columbia than the Nittinat word but the latter appears to have been in common use among the Nootkan related tribes. Both *peshak* and *mesachie* are acceptable and proper Jargon.

For the purpose of this argument we shall examine the ten words referred to in Jewitt's vocabulary, and then we shall take up Chinook dialect words contained in the book *Chinook Texts* by Dr. Franz Boas. We will find in both of these tribal dialects words which are also in the Jargon, either just as used by the Chinooks and the Nootkans in their own languages, or which, with slight and easily recognizable modifications, were taken from those dialects and converted into accepted and standard Jargon.

As these words were used by both the Nootkans and the Chinooks in their attempts to converse with the very first whites that came among them—notably Meares in 1788, Jewitt in 1803 and Lewis and Clark in 1804 and 1805—long before the advent of the Hudson's Bay or any other fur company, this circumstance would seem to fairly disprove the Hudson's Bay Company invention theory. What the Hudson's Bay Company did to the language—after it came into sole and supreme control of trading in this region—and all it did was to enlarge and enrich the Jargon and extend its use over the whole of its great Pacific Coast domain from Alaska to southern Oregon and from the ocean to the Rocky Mountains.

Jewitt's Nootkan vocabulary gives the word *klootzmah* for woman, *klootz-chem-up* for sister, *tenassis-kloots-mah* for daughter and *tenassis-check-up* for son. *Check-up* is man. (We have followed Jewitt's not very uniform spelling literally.)

In the Jargon *klootchman* is woman and *tenas* (short e) is lesser, little, younger. *Tenas klootchman* is little woman or daughter, and *tenas man* is son. *Man* is man in the Jargon. *Boston man* is American, due to the fact that the early ships trading on the coast came largely from Boston. Then, with the Hudson's Bay Company came the British influence, and *King Chautsh man* became Jargon for Englishman, *Chautsh* being the nearest approach to George the Indian was capable of.

There was another word that was a near equivalent then for person, whether man or woman. It was *tillikum*. Some writers of Alaska and northwest stories, who have heard the word, erroneously think it means friend or partner and would restrict it to indicate some very similar close personal friendship—a sort of super friendship. The proper word for friend is *sikhs*, pronounced six. *Tillikum* is used in that sense now, but was not so used originally.

Tillikum means people. The early Jargon and many of the dialects recognized but two groups—*tyee* and *tillikum*. Every authority from Gibbs to Shaw agrees on that. *Nesika tillikums* is our people. It is far-fetched to try to make the word mean some deep, subtle inner relationship. There are no subtleties of meaning either in the Jargon or in the dialects. An illustration of the flexibility of Chinook—the Jargon—and of the manner in which *sikhs* may be employed is found in the concluding phrase of *Told in the Hills* (1891) by Marah Ellis Ryan. That entertaining romance ends with the expression: *Klahowya opitsah.* It is meant to be an equivalent for "goodbye sweetheart" but is a wrong expression.

No special word for sweetheart or lover exists in the Jargon. *Opitsah* is literally "knife." So *klahowya opitsah* really was "goodbye *knife.*" If the author had had her hero say: *Klahowya opitsah sikhs* she would have used proper Jargon. *Opitsah sikhs* is literally "fork," friend of the knife. "Every knife has its fork," says Gill, so "*opitsah sikhs*" is made to do duty for sweetheart or lover.

Tyee is chief or ruler. In the Nootkan only the highest chief seems to have been a Tyee. In the Jargon *Saghalie Tyee* is God, literally the ruler of heaven, the chief above. The word is commonly pronounced as if it were spelled Sockalee.

Jewitt says the Nootkan for sky is *sie-yah.* In the Jargon *siah* is away, far off, remote. If very far, it is indicated by prolonging the last syllable, and if the speaker desires to indicate a very great distance indeed, he prolongs the word and separates the syllables to give almost the identical sound of Jewitt's spelling—*s-i-e—yah!* It is quite likely that sky to the Nootkans was the "very-far-off."

"No," according to Jewitt, is *wik.* Concomly said *waket* to Lewis and Clark. In the Jargon as it has been spoken for over a hundred years the word is *wake.* *Wake kumtux* is "don't understand."

Iron, says Jewitt, is *sick-a-miny.* *Chikamin* is Jargon for metal, but usually means money. The Indians knew nothing of paper as money; and accepted only silver and lesser coins.

Mamook-su-mah in Jewitt's vocabulary is an expression which means to go and fish, and to go and fish was work to the Indian, about the only work he knew. *Mamook* is Jargon for work or for any other performance—anything one does. *Mamook muckamuck* is to get the food ready, prepare it. *Ikta mika mamook* is "what are you doing?" *Cultus mamook* is bad work, evil deeds, doing the wrong thing or doing it in the wrong way. *Mamook kumtux* means to teach, literally to make known or to understand.

Chee-alt-see-klattur-wah is used in Jewitt's account as the equivalent of "go away." Go in the Chinook Jargon is just *klatawa*, and go away would be *klatawa siah*, or go yonder. It is probable that the string of suffixes Jewitt uses qualifies or enlarges the meaning of his *klattur-wah*.

Mahkook is to buy, sell, trade or exchange. It is one of the most used of Jargon expressions. Jewitt spells it *ma-kook* and limits the meaning to "to sell."

For "I understand" he uses the one word *kom-me-tak*. The proper Jargon for "I understand" is *Nika kumtux*. This is *kummatux* when spoken by a native Chinook, or was when there were any pure stock native Chinooks alive.

10. CHINOOK TEXTS OF FRANZ BOAS

BEFORE THIS INTERESTING NATIVE RACE—THE Lower Chinooks—lost their last identity some valuable work was done by Franz Boas in collecting and recording their myths and stories. These were published by the Bureau of Ethnology of the Smithsonian Institution under the title *Chinook Texts*, but are now out of print and copies are rare and difficult to obtain.

In 1891 Doctor Boas found only two people, Charles Cultee and Catherine, who could speak Chinook (the original language), living then at Bay Center, on Shoalwater Bay, among Chehalis Indians. From Cultee Dr. Boas learned and wrote a number of the original tribal tales or myths of the Indians of the Columbia. In his introduction to his book, Dr. Boas says:

The following texts were collected in the summers of 1890 and 1891. While studying the Salishan languages of Washington and Oregon I learned that the dialects of the Lower Chinook were on the verge of disappearing, and that only a

few individuals survived who remembered the languages of
the once powerful tribes of the Clatsop and Chinook. This fact
determined me to make an effort to collect what little remained
of these languages.

I first went to Clatsop, where a small band of Indians are
located near Seaside, Clatsop County, Oregon. Although a number of them belonged to the Clatsop tribe, they had all adopted
the Nehalim language, a dialect of the Salishan Tillamook. This
change of language was brought about by frequent intermar-
riages with the Nehalim. I found one middle-aged man and two
old women who still remembered the Clatsop language, but it
was impossible to obtain more than a vocabulary and a few
sentences. The man had forgotten a great part of the language,
while the women were not able to grasp what I wanted; they
claimed to have forgotten their myths and traditions, and
could not or would not give me any connected texts. One old
Clatsop woman, who had been married to a Mr. Smith, was
too sick to be seen, and died soon after my visit. The few remaining Clatsops had totally forgotten the history of their tribe,
and even maintained that no allied dialect was spoken north
of the Columbia River and on Shoalwater Bay (now Willapa
Harbor). They assured me that the whole country was occupied by the Chehalis, another Salishan tribe. They told me,
however, that a few of their relatives, who still continued to
speak Clatsop, lived on Shoalwater Bay among the Chehalis.

I went to search for this remnant of the Clatsop and Chinook
peoples, and found them located at Bay Center, Pacific County,
Washington. They proved to be the last survivors of the Chinook, who at one time occupied the greater part of Shoalwater
Bay and the northern bank of the Columbia River as far as
Grays Harbor. The tribe has adopted the Chehalis language in
the same way in which the Clatsop have adopted the Nehalim.
The only individuals who spoke Chinook were Charles Cultee
and Catherine. While I was unable to obtain anything from the
latter, Cultee proved to be a veritable storehouse of informa-

tion. His mother's mother was a Katlamat (Cathlamet) and his mother's father a Quilapax; his father's mother was a Clatsop, and his father's father a Tinneh of the interior. His wife is a Chehalis, and at present he speaks Chehalis almost exclusively, this being also the language of his children. He has lived for a long time in Katlamat, on the southern bank of the Columbia River, his mother's town, and for this reason speaks the Katlamet dialect as well as the Chinook dialect. He uses the former dialect in conversing with Samson, a Katlamat Indian, who is also located at Bay Center. Until a few years ago he spoke Chinook with one of his relatives, while he uses it now only rarely when conversing with Catherine, who lives a few miles from Bay Center. Possibly this Chinook is to a certain extent mixed with Katlamat expressions, but from a close study of the material I conclude that it is on the whole pure and trustworthy.

I have obtained from Cultee a series of Katlamat texts also, which appear to me not quite so good as the Chinook texts, but nevertheless give a good insight into the differences of the two dialects. It may be possible to obtain material in this dialect from other sources.

My work of translating and explaining the texts was greatly facilitated by Cultee's remarkable intelligence. After he had once grasped what I wanted, he explained to me the grammatical structure of the sentences by means of examples, and elucidated the sense of difficult periods.

This work was more difficult as we conversed only by means of the Chinook Jargon.

Boas's texts are written first in the pure Chinook dialect, as spoken by Cultee, with an accompanying literal translation, line for line, beneath the original. Each of the stories is followed by a free translation entirely in English.

These texts, as he relates, were told to him by Cultee, transcribed into the difficult and complex dialect of the original Chinook, translated literally and again in free form, all by means of the Jargon, which shows its marvelous flexibility. Though well over half of the words were derived from the Chinook, with contributions from the Nootkans, other tribal dialects represented include the Chehalis, Wasco, Klickitat, Clackamas, Bellabella, Cree, Clallam, and Calapooian. Added to these were words that imitated natural sounds, and words picked up from the French *voyageurs* and the English and American traders. The most guttural of the Jargon words are those which came from the dialects of the Chinookan tribes.

These facts do seem to show beyond any possibility of doubt that the Jargon came into existence during some long-past prehistoric period, as a polyglot of native words for use in intertribal commercial and trading intercourse, and that it was later enlarged to fit the requirements of trade when the fur companies established posts in the region.

The dominance of Chinook words also seems to indicate that the Chinook were, as the early explorers and traders repeatedly said, the dominant tribe of the Pacific between the 42nd and the 57th degrees of latitude.

This dominance of Chinook words in the Jargon doubtless made it easier for Dr. Boas to so faithfully record these texts. Study of them will show the marked present-day similarity of many Jargon words to the Lower Chinook dialect from which they came.

11. JARGON WORDS THAT COME FROM PURE CHINOOK

ON THE VERY FIRST PAGE OF BOAS's *Chinook Texts* we find an old friend, *alta*. It is pronounced "ahlta," both in the Jargon and in the original Chinook. It means "now," the present.

The next one is not so easily recognized because of Boas's attempt to give it the exact sound of Cultee's pronunciation — *smokst,* the equivalent of the numeral "two." It is *mokst* in the Jargon. *Kwanisum* (always) with a long "a" is pure Chinook; *kwonesum* with "o" pronounced "ah" is Jargon.

According to Shaw, *he-he*, the Jargon for laugh, is onomatopoeia, or the Indians' rude attempt to imitate sound; but Boas uses *he-he* as Chinook for laugh. We must accept the word, therefore, as of Chinook origin.

We find in the same text the strangely spelled word *ncitkum*. It is used for the expression, "I am half." Half in the Jargon is *sitkum*. Cultee probably pronounced it with a partial elision of the *n* sound and an explosive *s* sound for the *c*. In Jargon *sitkum dolla* is half a dollar. *Sitkum siwash* is half Indian, half breed, or literally half savage; as *siwash*, a generic term applied to all the Indians of the Northwest, is merely a corruption of the French word *sauvage*.

Farther along we find *kwanisum* again, but this time Boas spells it *kua-nEsum*, giving a "q" sound to the *ku*, a long "a" and uses the capital "E" to denote a partial elision of the sound of that vowel. *Kwanisum*, wherever he uses it, is the equivalent of always.

Now we come to *ikta* and find it used for both what and things. In the Jargon, *ikta* is what, becoming *iktas* for things.

Another old friend, rather uncouth in appearance, is a word he strangely spells *aiaq*. The meaning in Boas's translation is quick; so we readily recognize *hyak*, which is Jargon for quick, fast, hurry.

Then we encounter *naika*, the first personal pronoun "I" in Chinook, which in the Jargon is *nika*. Likewise it is used for me and my; and *mika* is you and yours, but is *maika* in the original and *mika* in the Jargon.

O-pol-e-ka, according to Boas, means night. The Jargon for night is simply *polaklie*—which also means darkness or gloom like night.

Boas gives *enatai* as the equivalent of across or on the other side, in Chinook. In the Jargon it loses a letter to become simply *enati*. He cites *kanauwe* as Chinook for all. The Jargon uses *konaway*. He gives *ikanim* for canoe; in the Jargon it is *canim*, long "a" and accent on the last syllable.

In Boas's, or Cultee's, *anqate*, long ago, we have no difficulty in recognizing *ahnkuttie*, Jargon for the same expression.

There are many others but these will be sufficient. Cultee was talking the language of the ancient Chinooks to Dr. Boas, a tongue that had been in use for untold centuries by an active, powerful, warlike, once-numerous trading tribe of intelligent Indians. These words are found alike in their dialects and in the Jargon. Their pronunciations have undergone some transformations, modified by long use among the many differing tribes and the half century or more of later contact with white traders, but there is not much doubt that more than half of the present Jargon vocabulary was in use as a primitive, prehistoric trading language long before these Indians knew that a white man or white race existed.

Concomly, chief of the Lower Chinooks, spoke words taken from the original Nootkan when he said, "*Waket commatux*" for "I do not understand" to Lewis and Clark in 1805. That was six years before there had been other than maritime traders on this coast, and sixteen years before there was a Hudson's Bay post anywhere on the shores of the Pacific.

One word in Meares's account of his experiences on the Northwest Coast in 1788, a phrase or two in the Journal of Lewis and Clark, ten words of the Nootkan vocabulary given by Jewitt, two others in the body of his Narrative—*Tyee* and *pechak*—and his discovery that the tribe had two languages (one he thought for purely poetical expression in their war songs and lyrics and the other for common use) show beyond doubt that the Jargon existed and was used by widely separated tribes, at least—going all the way back to Meares's quotation of the word *cloosh* spoken by Callicum—twenty-three years before the Astor party arrived at the mouth of the Columbia; for *kloshe* is original Chinook as well as Jargon and it was spoken by a Nootkan in 1788 off the west coast of Vancouver Island.

Callicum's use of the word was natural. He was talking to a stranger, a foreigner, a man from another tribe, even though the tribe was white. The Jargon was the common means of communication under such circumstances among all the hundreds of tribes and families of the whole vast region. The Nootkans used it in their relations with Jewitt for the same reason, and so did Concomly, the Chinook chief, or Tyee, in his attempt to talk to Lewis and Clark. That the whites could not respond in kind may have given the natives a poor opinion of the visitors' attainments. They may have felt that the whites lacked education, and from the Indian standpoint they did; but they respected the force of ships and firearms and the wealth of goods the ships and traders brought with them, and in time taught them the Jargon. At that point they all finally found a common ground, for they could communicate with each other.

Though there were many ships in the maritime trade prior to 1800 there was little contact before that with the natives. This accounts for the meagerness of the records. The ship masters cared only for furs. They cruised off shore during the summer, and the Indians came out to them in canoes. When all the trading was done the laden vessels sailed for the ports of China, or, if out for several years, wintered in the Sandwich Islands. These ship traders knew nothing of native customs, tribes or languages; cared nothing for them, had no interest in such squalid people except the trade they could carry on with them in the most primitive methods of exchange and barter.

It is for this reason that study of their logs and records offers so little evidence either for or against the prehistoric origin of the trade Jargon now known as Chinook.

12. NATIVE CONTRIBUTIONS TO THE JARGON

FOUR FAMILIES OF TRIBES ACCOUNT FOR MOST of the dialect words in the Jargon, notably the Chinookan, the Salish, the Wakashan and the Kwakiutl. The Chinook family, divided into many tribes with somewhat differing dialects, lived in the valley of the Columbia River from the Pacific Ocean up to the country of the

Klickitats. These tribes contributed the largest number of words to the Jargon.

The second in importance is the contribution of the Nootkan branch of the Wakashan group. Salish words are third and Kwakiutl are fourth in number.

The Chinook family—including the important tribes of the Cathlamet, the Clatsop, the Wasco, and the Klickitats—seems to have built the foundation of this coast trade language, and because of their intimate trade relations in prehistoric tribal days with the Nootkans, with whom they exchanged slaves for shell money, words from the Nootkans are second in number.

The Nootkans occupied the west coast of Vancouver Island and comprised the Nittinat, Clayoquots, Tokwhats, Makahs and many minor tribes. They were numerically strong, were warlike in character, possessed the trading instinct, and were daring seamen and skilled hunters. They lived on a stormy coast of the wildest nature, that was indented, however, by some excellent harbors to which the early explorers learned to come for shelter and in time used as a general rendezvous.

The Salish family lived on Grays Harbor, Willapa Harbor and on Puget Sound. The most important of these, so far as the formation of the Jargon is concerned, were the Chehalis, and after them the Nisqually and Lummi tribes.

The important Kwakiutl contributions came from the tribe now known as Bellabellas, but which in reality were the Heiltsuqs. They lived on and around Millbank Sound, on the inside passage to Alaska, which is to say on the inside of Vancouver Island, while the Ahts—the Nootkans and their allies—lived on the outside. Both the Ahts and the Kwakiutl were cannibals, but the practice was more general among the Kwakiutl than among the Nootkans, and persisted, too, among the former to a much later day. Slavery was practiced among all these natives—Chinook, Salish, Wakashan and Kwakiutl. The Jargon sprang directly from the necessities of this practice, as slaves were the basis of their trade relations.

13. SPELLING AND PRONUNCIATION OF CHINOOK

IN COMPILING THIS DICTIONARY THE AUTHOR
has aimed at a better uniformity of spelling. The early dictionaries
were written by men who, like Gibbs, went among the Indians and
acquired the Jargon from them. In different localities the natives
had different pronunciations. The words were written as they
sounded. As many of the early dictionaries were the work of teach-
ers, missionaries, writers and students of ethnological research the
result was as described by Eells. But in later years there has been
an effort at some sort of standardization. We feel that our spelling
is rational, that it represents the words as they are now pronounced
and that usage has given us a form to follow. We have tried to
follow it. As there are but few copies of older works on Chinook
to be found, even in the Northwest, where it was so widely used
not so long ago, we feel that the spelling adopted by this work will
prove acceptable to all who know the Jargon.

Following are two statements in regard to the spelling, pronunciation and arrangement of Chinook words.

The first is by Myron Eells, author of *Hymns in the Chinook Jargon*
(1878) and the *Manuscript Dictionary of the Chinook Jargon* (1893).
It is widely believed that the best examples of the literature written
in the Chinook Jargon may be found in the works of Eells, two selections from which appear in Chapter 12 of this book, "Chinook Jargon
as a Literary Language."

The different ways in which some words are spelled is a
curiosity and simply shows what educated men will do in this
line when they have no standard authority. Very seldom is any
word, even the simplest and easy one, spelled in the same way,
if it is found in several dictionaries, while some of them are
spelled in very many different ways . . . .

Other ways of spelling *kalakala: culacula; kallakala; kalah-
kalah; kilakila; kulakula; kullukala; cullaculla; cullerculler;*

cullacullah; kullakullie; kullukulli; kulakulla, etc. An exami-
nation of many dictionaries will show among other words—
konas, spelled in ten different ways: *ahnkuttie* and *keekwulee,*
each in twelve; *klootchman* and *kliminawhit,* each in fifteen;
klatawa, seeowist, and *memaloose,* each in sixteen; *tahtlum, kloshe,* and *killapi,* each in eighteen; and *kunsih*
in nineteen different ways; *deaub* is in twelve ways, and *ooahut*
in fourteen, but they show a wide variety of sound, *deaub* being
also *dahblo, diaub, derb, leiom,* and *yaub;* and *ooahut* being
hooihut, wayhut, wehkut, and *oyhut.* Even words which are
derived from the English generally have different spellings as
soon as the standard English authority is left, so that *glease* from
grease becomes *gleese, gleece, glis,* and *klis; bed* is also spelled
pet; moon is also *mun; nose* is also *nos; stone* is also *ston; stocking* is also *stocken, staken,* and *stoken; Sunday* is also *sante; tea*
is also *ti; pepah* (paper) is also *papeh, paper, paypa, papah,
pepah, pepa,* and *peppah;* and warm also is spelled *waum, wam,
wahm,* and *wawm. Shot, skin, man,* and a few others have for
almost a wonder found no other way of being spelled.

There are three reasons for this difference in spelling—which
may occur even though the same sound of the letters is pre-
served; thus *wam* may be *waum* or *wawm* and still preserve the
same sound of *a.* Again, when any writer adopts a regular
schedule of sounds for each vowel, he will surely differ in spelling from those who attempt to follow as near as possible the
English mode of spelling. Boas, St. Onge, and to a considerable
degree Durieu have done this, hence *tea* becomes *ti; poolie, puli,*
and so on.

Still farther, different modes of pronunciation in different
localities, and sometimes in the same locality, are the cause of
different ways of spelling. This is especially seen in the words
already referred to, *ooahut* and *deaub;* so *kloshe* becomes *tlush*
or *tloos,* and also a large number beginning with *kl* begin with
tl in another place; *tahlkie* becomes *tahnlkie,* and so on. Sometimes indeed it is very difficult to discover the true sound, as

for instance, whether the first syllable of *kalakala* should be spelled with an *a* or *u*, or the last one of *tukamonuk* with an *a* or *u*, and so on. The mode of pronunciation, and hence the mode of spelling, has undoubtedly changed somewhat since Parker in 1835-6 wrote the first vocabulary. Hence in comparing the ways of spelling the reader ought to remember the place where, the date when, and the system of pronunciation, especially of vowel sounds adopted by each writer. . . .

There is no settled authority in regard to the order of the words in this language. They are generally placed in much the same order as they are in the language which the speaker has been accustomed to use, if he be not well acquainted with the language. An English speaking person will place them in much the same order that he would in English, but there are many phrases where this is not true, the order of which must be acquired by practice: for instance,—*halo nika kumtuks*,—not I understand, is far more common than *nika halo kumtuks*. An Indian who has learned somewhat the English order, will arrange the words in much the same way; but if the speaker is an old Indian who knows but little about English he will arrange them much as he is accustomed to do in his native tongue, which is usually very different from the English. As the tendency, however, is not for the whites to learn the native Indian languages, but for the Indians to learn the English, so the tendency is toward the English order of the words.

The additional two paragraphs below, the first dealing with the orthography and the second with the pronunciation of Chinook, are by Horatio Hale. Hale was the philologist with the Charles Wilkes scientific expedition that visited the Columbia and the Willamette Valley during the year 1841:

As will be seen, the orthography of the Jargon is unsettled and capricious. Most writers spell Indian and French words "by the ear," but use the ordinary English spelling for the English words comprised in the language, without regard to uniformity. . . . Some writers, however, retain in the Jargon the "digraph" *gh*, to express, in some words of Chinook origin, the sound of the German guttural *ch* in *Buch.* . . .

As the Jargon is to be spoken by Englishmen and Frenchmen, and by Indians of at least a dozen tribes, so as to be alike easy and intelligible to all, it must admit no sound which cannot be readily pronounced by all. The numerous harsh Indian gutturals either disappear entirely, or are softened to *h* and *k* . . . On the other hand, the *d, f, g, r, v, z*, of the English and French become in the mouth of a Chinook, *t, p, k, l, w*, and *s. The* English j, (dzh), is changed to *ch,* (tsh). The French nasal *n* is dropped or is retained without its nasal sound.

Eells respected the work done by Hale on the Chinook Jargon but felt the latter "labored under the disadvantage of not having mingled much with those who have used the language for about fifty years." With Eells it was far different. He had spent a lifetime mingling with them.

14. CHINOOK JARGON AS A LITERARY LANGUAGE*

> A Chinook word is elastic and expresses a broad and general idea rather than one altogether specific, hence the extreme elasticity of the Chinook jargon.   BUCHANAN

"A grotesque jargon called Chinook is the lingua-franca of the whites and Indians of the Northwest," wrote Theodore Winthrop in 1853. "It is a jargon of English, French, Spanish, Chinook, Kallapooga, Haida, and other tongues, civilized and savage. It is an attempt on a small scale to nullify Babel by combining a confusion of tongues into a confounding of tongues—a witches' caldron in which the vocable that bobs up may be some old familiar Saxon verb, having suffered Procrustean docking or elongation, and now doing

---

*From *History of Oregon Literature* (Metropolitan Press 1935) by Alfred Powers. Variations here in Jargon spelling are typical. The writers expressed how the words sounded to them. However, most of these variations are superficial; the basic sounds generally come through.

substantive duty; or some strange monster, evidently nurtured within the range of tomahawks and calumets. There is some danger that the beauties of this dialect will be lost to literature. The Chinook jargon still expects its poet."

To a surprisingly extensive and varied degree it is not lost to literature. And, as several selections will show, it has had its poets.

Altogether in a literary way it is an impressive language. Perhaps no other composite and manufactured tongue has served such noble and poetic purposes of expression. The missionaries used it as the successful medium for the communion of the spirits of two different peoples. From wilderness camps, hymns and prayers went up to God in the blue heaven above in the Chinook Jargon, which had a sufficient richness and flexibility for this exaltation and praise. Vast and magnificent it must have been, and very beautiful, as it came from tribal throats. A greater triumph it was for the Chinook Jargon than for Christian doctrine, considering that, as at the 1839 camp meeting at The Dalles, the Indians sometimes naively proposed that they ought to be paid for their excellent demonstrations of worship.

With more sincerity, an Indian girl used it for a death wail—a song of hope and immortality, with its beautiful refrain of *Tamala, tamala*—tomorrow and tomorrow. The last words of a Yakima chief were uttered in this tongue. When we read the dying expression of Stonewall Jackson—"Let us cross over the river and rest under the shade of the trees"—we realize what a beautiful language English is, when kept beautiful in its simplicity. So when Chief Qualchien in a quarter of an hour's time faced dark extinction, he cried out in Chinook Jargon a plea that reverberated in the recollection of an American soldier all his life as having the profoundest pathos of any sounds he ever heard. From its initial utilization as the parlance of barter to such uses as these, how far had the language advanced!

It was such a language that Myron Eells could say of it that for eighteen years he had "talked in it, sung in it, prayed and preached in it, translated considerable into it and thought in it. . . ."

Thought in it! For a white man it had become a vehicle of thought. To the lips of the Indian it came spontaneously to express his deepest feelings. Though the vocabulary was derived from many sources, the Indian's mind and spirit were the sieve through which it was strained. His was the governing philology. This kept it simple. This accounts for the child-like freshness and charm of the word combinations. This, in short, is what made it a literary language instead of a harsh, emotionless and artificial esperanto.

Much of the poetry of the Chinook Jargon comes from the application of a single adjective to an assortment of nouns to form by this combination new nouns instead of having separate substantives. For instance, take *tenas*, an adjective meaning small. Then take this list of nouns: *snass*—rain, *waum*—warm, *cole*—cold, *moos-moos*—cow, *klootchman*—woman. Then *tenas snass* would be a shower—little rain; *tenas waum* would be spring and *tenas cole* would be autumn—the season when it was getting a little warm or a little cold; *tenas moosmoos*, a small cow or a calf, and *tenas klootchman*, a small woman or a girl. How much more charming these synthetic phrases are than separate terms, as in a richer language, since the source of the meaning is right there with all its original atmosphere.

The Jargon gets a poetic quality from another child-like characteristic—that of onomatopoeia. ". . . most of the words," said Hezekiah Butterworth, "resemble in sounds the objects they represent. For example, a wagon in Chinook is *chick-chick*, a clock is *ding-ding*, a crow is *kaw-kaw;* a duck, *quack-quack;* a laugh, *tee-hee;* the heart is *tum-tum*, and a talk or a speech or sermon, *wah-wah*." It is not true, of course, that most words are of this nature, but the list given by Butterworth could be greatly extended from any Chinook Jargon dictionary.

It is a language that "has served as an inter-communicating medium between civilization and the mystery of the savage mind for more years than most people know." And before that it was serving as a linguistic clearing house for the savages of many dialects themselves. Interest in the Chinook Jargon is indicated by the fact that there have been more than fifty editions of vocabularies during the past hundred years.

The statement was made in *Oregon Native Son* in 1900 that "in pioneer days there were but few but what understood this language, and the children frequently could speak it as well as they could English."

The following examples of literature in the Chinook Jargon have been selected to represent most of the forms that could be found—hymns, sermons, prayers, translations, songs, poetry, dialogues, harangues, a letter, and the sad death plea of Qualchien. As Myron Eells noted, "The different ways in which some words are spelled is a curiosity and simply shows what educated men will do in this line when they have no standard authority."

Chinook Sermon to the Indians in 1888
By Myron Eells

About a fourth of the sermon, consisting of the first four paragraphs, is given here. The speaker used large pictures to which he referred in his discourse.

Moxt Sunday ahnkuttie nika memook kumtux mesika kopa okoke papeh. Yahwa mesika nanitch moxt klootchmen. Klaska chaco kopa mimaloose-illahee, kah Jesus mitlite, kopa Sunday, kopa delate tenas sun. Spose klaska klap okoke mimaloose-illahee, klaska halo nanitch Jesus. Jesus get-up; yaka klatawa. Kahkwa nika wawa kopa mesika talkie Sunday.

Okoke sun nika tikegh wawa kopa mesika kopa okoke papeh. Kimtah Jesus yaka get-up, yaka mitlite kopa illahee lakit tahtlum sun. Spose kopet lakit tahtlum sun, Jesus yaka tikegh klatawa kopa Saghalie. Kahkwa yaka lolo yaka tillikums klahanie kopa town, kopa okoke illahee kah mesika nanitch klaska. Yahwa mesika nanitch Jesus. Yahwa yaka tillikums. Jesus yaka tikegh potlatch kloshe wawa kopa yaka tillikums, elip yaka killapi kopa Saghalie.

Alta nika mamook kumtux mesika kopa Jesus yaka wawa kope yaka tillikums. Yaka wawa kopa klaska: "Kloshe mesika klatawa kopa konoway, illahee, konoway kah, pe lolo Bible wawa kopa konoway tillikums." Kahkwa Jesus yaka wawa kopa klaska.

Jesus yaka kumtux konoway tillikums, konoway kah, halo kumtux kopa kloshe home kopa Saghalie. Klaska halo kumtux kopa. Lejaub yaka home kopa hias piah. Jesus yaka kumtux ikt man yaka tumtum delate hias mahkook; yaka elip hias mahkook kopa konoway dolla pe konoway iktas kopa konoway illahee. Kahkwa yaka tikegh yaka tillikums, yaka leplet, klatawa konoway kah, pe help konoway tillikums mash Lejaub yaka owakut, pe klap Jesus yaka owakut.

TRANSLATION

Two Sundays ago I spoke to you concerning that picture. There you saw two women coming to the sepulchre where Jesus lay, on Sunday, just at sunrise, Jesus had risen; He was gone. So I told you in that sermon.

Today I wish to explain to you about this picture. After Jesus had risen, He continued on the earth forty days. When the forty days were ended, He desired to ascend to heaven. So he led the people out of the city to that place where you behold them. Here you see Jesus. There are those people. Jesus wished to give good instructions to the people before He returned to heaven.

Now I will explain to you the teaching of Jesus to those people. He said to them: "It is good that you should go to every country in all the world, and carry the Gospel to all nations." Thus spoke Jesus to them.

Jesus was aware that all the nations of the world had no knowledge of the Gospel. They knew nothing of the happy home in heaven. They knew nothing of the Devil's home in the great fire. Jesus knew that the soul of a man is truly precious; that it is more precious than all the money and everything else in the world. So He wished His people, His missionaries, to go everywhere, and to help all the people to leave the Devil's way, and to find the way of Jesus.

A Blessing Before Meals

By Myron Eells

O Saghalie Tyee, nesika Papa, nesika
O   God   our Father,   we
wawa mahsie kopa mika, mika potlach
say   thanks   to   thee, thou hast given
kopa nesika okoke muckamuck. Kloshe spose
to   us   this   food.   Good   if
mika kwanesum potlach muckamuck kopa
thou   always   will give   food   to
nesika. Kloshe spose mika potlatch mika
us.   Good   if thou   will give thy
wawa kopa nesika, kahkwa muckamuck kopa
words to   us,   as   food   to the
tumtum. Help nesika tumtum chaco kloshe.
mind.   Help   our   minds become good.
Kopa   Jesus nesika tikegh konoway okoke.
Through Jesus we   wish   all this.
Kloshe kahkwa.
Good   so.

The Ten Commandments

By Laura B. Downey Bartlett

Laura Bell Downey Bartlett, who came across the plains as a baby in 1853, is author of two books on the Chinook jargon— *Chinook-English Songs*, published in Portland in 1914, and *Dictionary of the Intertribal Language Commonly Called Chinook*, published in Tacoma in 1924.

1. *Nika Sah-ah-lie Tyee kopa mica.*
   I am the Lord thy God.
   Kopit ikt mika kumtux Sah-ah-lie Tyee.
   Thou shalt have no other Gods before me.

2. *Wake cultus wau-wau, Sah-ah-lie Tyee nem.*
   Thou shalt not take the name of the Lord thy God in vain.

3. *Kloash nanitch kwanisum sacra kopa Sunday.*
   Remember the Sabbath day to keep it holy.

4. *Kloash kumtux mika Papa pee mika Mama.*
   Honor thy Father and thy Mother.

5. *Wake mamook mamaloose klaxta.*
   Thou shalt not kill.

6. *Wake mamook ikta shem kopa mika itlwillie, pee kopa klaxta.*
   Thou shalt not commit adultery.

7. *Wake kapswalla.*
   Thou shalt not steal.

8. *Wake Kleminawhit.*
   Thou shalt not lie.

9. *Wake kumtux, pee wake tikegh ict shem kopa holoima klootch-man.*
   Thou shalt not covet thy neighbor's house, his wife or servants.

10. *Wake tikegh klaxta mika tikegh ikta.*
    Thou shalt not covet that which is not thine.

HYMN
By Daniel Lee and J. H. Frost

1. *Ak-ah eg-lah-lam en-si-kah*
   Mi-kah Ish-tam-ah em-e-hol-ew
   Kup-et mi-kam toke-ta mi-mah
   Mi-kah ek-ah-tlah gum-ohah
   Mi-kah dow-ah gum-e oh

Kon-a-wa e-toke-ta ten-mah
Mi-kah an-kut-e gum-toh.

Here we now unite in singing
Glory, Lord, unto thy name,
Only good and worthy praising,
Thou art always, Lord, the same.
Of the sun thou art Creator,
And the light was made by thee,
All things good, yea, every creature,
At the first thou madest to be.

2. *Mi-kah minch-ah koke en-si-kah*
   An-kut-e yuk-um-a-lah
   Kon-a-wa e-dinch ah-gu-it-quah
   Quon-sim po-nan-a-kow
   Mi-kah gum-inch-e-lute e-me-han
   Yok-ah wa-wot gach-o-weet
   Uk-ah en-si-kah quot-lanch-ke-hah
   Mi-kam toke-ta can-neo-eeb

   We, O Lord, are all thy children,
   In the past we wicked were,
   We were all most deeply wretched,
   Always blind and in despair;
   Thou didst thy Son our Savior,
   He to us instruction gave.
   Knowing this, we now are happy,
   Thou are good and thou wilt save.

"Whiskey"
Tune—"Bounding Billows"

1. *Ahnkuttie nika tikegh whiskey,*
   Pe alta nika mash.
   Alta nika mash.

Formerly I loved whiskey,
But now I throw it away—
Now I throw it away.

2. *Whiskey hias cultus,*
   Pe alta nika mash—
   Alta nika mash—
   Whiskey is good for nothing,
   And now I throw it away—
   Now I throw it away.

3. *Whiskey mimoluse tillikums,*
   Pe alta nika mash—
   Alta nika mash.
   Whiskey kills people,
   And now I throw it away—
   Now I throw it away.

4. *Cultus klaska muckamuck,*
   Pe alta nika mash—
   Alta nika mash.
   They that drink it, drink what is worthless,
   And now I throw it away—
   Now I throw it away.

From "Canoe and Saddle"

By Theodore Winthrop

Theodore Winthrop, a 25-year-old Yale graduate, spent the summer of 1853 in the Pacific Northwest, visiting Puget Sound, Portland, The Dalles, Oregon City, Salem, Marysville, Yoncalla, Scottsburg and St. Helens. Returning to New York, he studied law and was admitted to the bar, but devoted himself almost entirely to literary work, completing the five books which were published after his death in the Civil War in 1861. The best known of these is *Canoe and Saddle* (Nisqually edition, Binfords & Mort, Publishers) from which the following two selections were taken:

"Me No Like White Man Nohow"

The speaker was a root-digging Klickitat, called Shabbiest, because of
the shabby cast-off Christian coat he wore and little else. "At last . . . he
turned to me, and, raising his arms, one sleeveless, one fringed with rags
at the shoulder, delivered at me a harangue, in the most jerky and broken
Chinook. Given in broken English, its purport was as follows—in a naso-
guttural choke:"

What you white man want get 'em here? Why him no stay
Boston country? Me stay my country; no ask you come here. Too
much soldier man go all around everywhere. Too much make pop-
gun. Him say kill bird, kill bear—sometime him kill Indian. Soldier
man too much shut eye, open eye at squaw. Squaw no like; s'pose
squaw like, Indian man no like nohow. Me no understand white
man. Plenty good thing him country; plenty blanket; plenty gun;
plenty powder; plenty horse. Indian country plenty nothing. No
good Weenas give you horse. No good Loolowcan go Dalles. Bad
Indians there. Small-pox there. Very much all bad. Me no like
white man no-how. S'pose go away, me like. . . .

"Owhhigh, the Trader"

Theodore Winthrop was at the Hudson's Bay Post at Nisqually in need of
a guide through Indian country. It was arranged that the son of the famed
and crafty Indian trader, Owhhigh, be that guide. Winthrop wrote:

Now, however, Owhhigh, dropping in unceremoniously, laid aside his
sham dignity with a purpose. We had before agreed upon the terms of
payment for my guide. The ancient horse-thief sat like a Pacha, smoking
an inglorious dhudeen, and at last, glancing at certain articles of raiment of
mine, thus familiarly, in Chinook, broke silence.

Owhhigh. *"Halo she collocks nika tenas;* no breeches hath my son."
(the guide)

I. (in an Indianesque tone of some surprise, but great indifference) *"Ah hagh!"*

Owhhigh. *"Pe halo shirt;* and no shirt."

I. (assenting with equal indifference) *"Ah hagh!"*

Owhhigh smokes, and is silent, and Spokane Adonis fugues in,
"Pe wake yaka shoes; and no shoes hath he."

Another aide-de-camp takes up the strain. *"Yahwah mitlite shoes, clos he copa Owhhigh tenas;* there are shoes (pointing to a pair of mine) good for the son of Owhhigh."

I. *"Stick shoes ocock,—wake Closhe copa siwash;* hard shoes (not moccasins) those,—not good for Indian."

Owhhigh. *"Hyas tyee mika,—hin mitlite ikta,—halo ikta mitlite copa nika tenas,—mika tikky him potlatch;* great chief thou,—with thee plenty traps abide,—no traps hath my son,—thou wilt give him abundance."

I. *Pe hyas tyee Owhhigh,—conoway ikta mitlite-pe hin yaka potlatch copa liticum;* and a great chief is Owhhigh,—all kinds of property are his, and many presents does he make to his people."

Profound silence followed these mutual hints. . . . The choir bore their failure stoically. They had done their best that their comrade might be arrayed at my expense. . . . At last, to please Owhhigh, and requite him for the entertainment of his oratory, I promised that, if his son were faithful, I would give him a generous premium, possibly the very shirt and other articles they had admired. . . .

Nesika Wa-wa

A Chinook Letter from Yoncalla

Here we find the jargon used for business correspondence. What the letter says will be left for the reader to decipher for himself—it might furnish an hour of pleasant occupation. It was printed in the *Oregon Native Son* in September, 1900, with this explanatory statement: "Several of our subscribers became somewhat alarmed over the non-appearance of the last issue of the *Native Son* at its usual date of delivery, and wrote asking as to the reason why they did not receive it. Among those enquiring about the delay was one of our agents. Her message was as follows:"

Yoncalla, Oregon, August 8th, 1900.

Native Son Pub. Co.,

Klose Tenas Man:—Klone moon o'koke mika papah wake chaco copa conomox o'coke kloochman, Mrs. Susan Smith, *pee ole man* C. H. Westernheiser, Yoncalla. *Nesika hyas mesahche, copa nesika*

*spose mika wake copa yaka. Klose mika hyas mamook chaco o'koke
papah, copa skookum chickamin kuitan, pee klonas mesika kokshut
klose tumtum.*

Mike Klose Tilicum,
Sue Burt, Agent.

Lilly Dale in Chinook
(1852)

This is from the *Oregon Native Son* for July, 1899. "Lilly Dale," the sad
favorite of the mid-nineteenth century, was written by H. S. Thompson and
contains five stanzas and the chorus. The whole song was rendered into
Jargon, but only the first stanza and the chorus will be given here:

Hyas klose polikely kliminilimin tocope,
Mitlite klose konawa kah;
Pe yacka tillicum mitlite memaluse bed,
Nika kilihium, Lilly Dale.

Chorus:

O Lilly, *klose* Lilly, *hyas klose* Lilly Dale,
Alta tipso mitlite kopa kacka tenas memaluse house,
Kekwilla stick pe tipso klose illahee.

'Twas a calm still night and the moon's pale light
Shone soft o'er hill and vale;
When friends mute with grief, stood around the death bed
Of my poor, lost Lilly Dale.

Chorus:

O Lilly, sweet Lilly, dear Lilly Dale,
Now the wild rose blossoms o'er her little green grave
'Neath the trees in the flow'ry vale.

Tamala, Tamala
By Hezekiah Butterworth

"It was sunset on the bluffs and the valleys of the Columbia. . . . Among
the craft of the fishermen glided a long airy canoe, with swift paddles. It
contained an old Umatilla Indian, his daughter, and a young warrior. The

party were going to the young chief's funeral. As the canoe glided on amid
the still fishermen of other tribes, the Indian maiden began to sing. It was
a strange song, of immortality, and of spiritual horizons beyond the visible
life. The Umatillas have poetic minds. . . . She sang in Chinook, and the
burden of her song was that horizons will lift forever in the unknown
future. The Chinook word *tamala* means 'tomorrow'; and tomorrow, to the
Indian mind, was eternal life. . . . The thought of the song was something
as follows:"

Aha! it is ever tomorrow, tomorrow—
  Tamala, tamala, sing as we row;
Lift thine eye to the mount; to the wave give thy sorrow;
  The river is bright, and the rivulets flow;
      Tamala, tamala,
      Ever and ever;
The morrows will come and the morrows will go—
      Tamala! Tamala!

Happy boat, it is ever tomorrow, tomorrow—
  Tamala, whisper the waves as they flow;
The crags of the sunset the smiles of light borrow,
  As soft from the ocean the Chinook winds blow:
      Tamala, tamala,
      Ever and ever;
The morrows will come and the morrows will go—
      Tamala! Tamala!

Aha! the night comes, but the light is tomorrow—
  Tamala, tamala, sing as we go;
The waves ripple past, like the heart-beats of sorrow,
  And the boat beats the wave to our song as we row;
      Tamala, tamala,
      Ever and ever;
The morrows will come and the morrows will go—
      Tamala! Tamala!

For ever and ever horizons are lifting—
  Tamala, tamala, sing as we row;
And life toward the stars of the ocean is drifting,
  Through death will the morrow all endlessly glow—

Tamala! tamala!
Ever and ever;
The morrows will come and the morrows will go,
Tamala! Tamala!

Death Plea of Chief Qualchien

This pathetic and futile plea is given in B. F. Manring's *Conquest of the Coeur d' Alenes, Spokanes and Palouses.* Qualchien was a chief of the Yakimas. He rode voluntarily into the camp of Colonel George Wright. He was decked out in scarlet and at his belt hung an ornamented tomahawk and pistol. With him was his squaw, daughter of the Spokane chief, striking in her beauty and richly attired. He was accompanied by a brave and followed by a hunchback. He presented in general a dashing air. Then came the swift and abject change. He was made captive and sentenced to be hanged, and within fifteen minutes of his appearance in camp he was dead. He was completely overcome by the unexpected and sudden sentence. He prostrated himself upon the ground and then struggled as he was dragged forward, all the while "imploring them most piteously not to hang him. To General Lyon in later years, is attributed the declaration that no more mournful sounds were ever heard than those made by Qualchien in begging for his life. Over and over he repeated:"

Kopet, sikhs! Kopet, sikhs! Wake memaloose nika! Nika potlatch hiyu chikamin, hiyu kuitan, spose mika wake memaloose nika! Hiyu siwash solleks!

Stop, friends! Stop, friends! Don't kill me! I will give you a lot of money and many horses if you will not kill me! Many Indians will be angry!

The Lord's Prayer

The following version of the Lord's Prayer shows the lack of adaptation of the Jargon to any but the simplest use, yet it also has a pathos in its rudeness and poverty. How incomplete, even in our English, is the idea we get from the words, "Thy kingdom come!" This version of the "Lord's Prayer" is nearly the same as that prepared by a priest for McCormick's Chinook Dictionary (1852).

Nesika	Papa	klaksta	mitlite	kopa	Saghalie,	kloshe	kopa
Our	Father	who	dwellest	in the	above,	sacred	in

nesika	tumtum	mika	nem.	Nesika	hiyu	ticky
our	hearts (be)	Thy	name.	We	greatly	long for

chako	mika	illahee.	Mamook	mika	kloshe	tumtum
the coming of Thy kingdom.			Do	Thy	good	will

kopa	okoke	illahee, kahkwa	kopa	Saghalie.	Potlatch
with	this	world, as also	in the heavens.		Give (us)

konaway	sun	nesika	muckamuck,	pe	mahlie
day by day		our	bread,	and remember not	

konaway	nesika	mesachie,	kahkwa	nesika	mamook
all	our	wickedness,	even as	we	do also

kopa	klaska	spose	mamook	mesachie	kopa	nesika.
with	others	if they	do	evil	unto ourselves.	

Wake	lolo	nesika	kopa	peshak,	pe	mahsh siah
Not	bring	us	into	danger,	but	put far away

kopa	nesika	konoway	mesachie.
from	us	all	evil.

Kloshe kahkwa.
So may it be.

15. CONVERSATIONAL PHRASES

The brief examples here, together with the phrases following words in the Chinook-English vocabulary, illustrate the use of the Jargon as completely as possible in limited space and with such a condensed idiom. The absence of the minor parts of speech and inflected forms makes the combination of words in sentences either circuitous or bluntly direct.

English	*Chinook*
Good morning.	Klahowya.
Good evening.	
Good day.	
Good-by.	
How do you do?	
Good morning, friend.	Klahowya, sikhs.
Come here.	Chako yukwa.
How are you?	Kahta mika?
Are you sick?	Sick na mika?
Are you hungry?	Olo na mika?
Are you thirsty?	Olo na chuck mika?
How did you come?	Kahta mika chako?
What's the matter?	Ikta mamook?

English	Chinook
Would you like something to eat?	Mika ticky muckamuck?
Do you want work?	Mika ticky mamook?
What do you want to do?	Ikta mika mamook?
Cut some wood.	Mamook stick.
Certainly.	Nowitka.
How much do you want for cutting that lot of wood?	Kunsih dolla spose mika mamook konaway okoke stick?
One dollar.	Ikt dolla.
That is too much. I will give half a dollar.	Hyas mahkook. Nika potlatch sitkum dolla.
No! Give three quarters.	Wake! Potlatch klone kwata.
Very well; get to work.	Kloshe kahkwa; mamook alta.
Where is the ax?	Kah lahash?
There it is.	Yahwa.
Cut it small for the stove.	Mamook tenas, spose chikamin piah.
Give me a saw.	Potlatch lasee.
I have no saw; use the ax.	Nika halo lasee; iskum lahash.
All right.	Nowitka.
Bring it inside.	Lolo yaka kopa house.
Where shall I put it?	Kah nika mahsh okoke?
There.	Yahwa.
Here is something to eat.	Yukwa mitlite mika muckamuck.
Here is some bread.	Yahkwa mitlite piah sapolil.
Now bring some water.	Alta klatawa iskum chuck.
Where shall I get it?	Kah nika iskum?
In the river there.	Kopa cooley chuck yahwa.
Make a fire.	Mamook piah.
Boil the water.	Mamook liplip chuck.
Cook the meat.	Mamook piah okoke itlwillie.
Wash the dishes.	Mamook wash okoke leplah.
In what?	Kopa kahta?
In that pan.	Kopa okoke ketling.
Come again tomorrow.	Chako weght tomolla.
Come here, friend.	Chako yukwa, sikhs.
What do you want?	Ikta mika ticky?
I want you to do a little job in the morning.	Nika ticky mika mamook tenas mamook tenas sun.
Come very early.	Chako elip sun.
Come here at six o'clock.	Chako yukwa taghum tintin.
Oh! here you are!	Alah! Mika chako!
What do you want me to do?	Ikta mika ticky nika mamook?
Carry this box to the steamer.	Lolo okoke lacaset kopa piah ship.
Take this bag, also.	Lolo weght lesac.
What will you pay?	Ikta mika potlatch dolla?
A quarter.	Ikt kwata.

English	Chinook
Very well; and something to eat?	Kloshe kahkwa; pe tenas mucka-muck?
It is pretty heavy.	Hyas till okoke.
Is that man your brother?	Yaka na mika kaupho okoke man?
Can't he help you carry the box?	Na yaka mamook elan mika lolo lecaset?
I will give him something, too.	Nika potlatch weght tenas yaka.
Can you carry it?	Na, skookum kopa mika lolo okoke?
Is it very heavy?	Hyas till okoke?
Oh, no! We shall do it.	Wake! Nesika mamook.
Are you tired?	Mika chako till?
How far is it, this ship?	Kunsih siah, okoke ship?
Not much farther.	Wake siah alta.
That is all.	Kopet.
Do you understand English?	Kumtux mika Boston wawa?
No, not very much.	Wake hiyu.
Will you sell that fish?	Mika ticky mahsh okoke pish?
Which of them?	Klaksta?
That large one.	Okoke hyas.
What is the price of it?	Kunsih chikamin ticky?
I'll give you two bits.	Nika potlatch mokst bit.
I'll give you half a dollar.	Nika potlatch sitkum dolla.
No, that is not enough.	Wake, okoke wake hiyu.
Where did you catch that trout?	Kah mika iskum okoke tzum sam-mon?
In Skamokaway river.	Kopa Skamokaway cooley chuck.
Are there many fish there?	Na hiyu pish yahwa?
Not many; too much logging.	Wake; mamook alta hiyu stick.
Well, I won't buy it today.	Abba, nika wake ticky mahkook okoke sun.
What do you think of this country?	Ikta mika tumtum okoke illahee?
It is very pleasant when it does not rain.	Hyas kloshe hyas spose wake snass.
Not always; it is worse when it snows and freezes	Wake kwonesum. Chako kimtah klo-she spose cole snass pe shelipo.
How long have you lived here? (how many years)	Kunsih cole mitlite yahkwa mika?
Many years; I forget how many.	Hiyu cole; kopet kumtux kunsih.
I was born at Skipanon.	Chee tenas nika kopa Skipanon.
Did you get your wife here?	Na mika iskum mika klootchman yaka?
No; she is a Tillamook woman. I married her at Nehalem.	Wake; Tillamook klootchman. Nika mallie yaka kopa Nehalem.
How many children have you?	Kunsih tenas mika?

English	Chinook
We have three boys and one little girl.	Nesika klone tenas man nesika pe ikt tenas klootchman.
I will send you some things for them when I get home.	Nika mahsh mika iktas kopa kaska kimta ko nika illahee.

CHARLES CULTEE (Kwelte)

Last known survivor of the ancient Chinook stock

It was Cultee who gave Dr. Franz Boas the material for his *Chinook
Texts*, published by the Smithsonian Institution, Bureau of Ethnology,
in 1894. Material was gathered by Dr. Boas in the summers of 1890
and 1891. They communicated with each other entirely in the Chinook
Jargon. Note Cultee's flattened head.

Part Two: A DICTIONARY

GRAMMAR OF THE JARGON

IT MAY NOT, AT FIRST, BE EASY TO UNDERSTAND how a language composed of so few words could have been used so widely as the sole medium of communication among many thousands of individuals. However, a thorough knowledge of a few dozen basic words of the Jargon will give one sufficient material with which, after a little practice, to carry on actual conversations. The unique faculty of the Jargon for combining and compounding simple words and sounds makes it capable of almost unlimited expression.

Just as a child builds houses from blocks, so does the speaker of the Jargon build sentences by skillful combining of words and sounds. To a great extent, effective communication through the Jargon depends upon the ingenuity and imagination of the speaker.

There are no hard and fast rules for the spelling of words in the Chinook Jargon, and everyone, in writing Chinook, follows the dictates of his own judgment in the fabrication of phonetic equivalents, which are at best only approximations. The Chinook Jargon is essentially a spoken and not a written tongue . . . it is very much alive!

The Chinook Jargon is absolutely inflexible. It never changes its form for mood, tense, or anything else. The same form is used generally for both singular and plural, though occasionally an "s" is added to indicate the plural.

The idea of time is conveyed by adding a word to indicate it. Thus, past, present and future are usually indicated by these three words: ahnkuttie, alta, and alki. Ordinarily, if the time is omitted or not specified, it is understood to be present time. For example:

53

"Nika kumtux ahnkuttie"— I understood, I understood some time ago.

"Nika kumtux alta"—I understand now (or just "nika kumtux" —I understand).

"Nika kumtux alki"— I will understand, I will understand by and by, I will understand after while.

Intensity of meaning or duration of time may also be indicated by prolongation of the sounding of the word, thus: Laly (time) would be pronounced la-a-a-aly to suggest a long time. This is based upon an instinctive principle common to all tongues, just as we in English phonetically indicate prolongation of time or extension in space or intensity of feeling by means of prolonging "a long time" into "a lo-o-o-o-ng time." The days of the week and the number of weeks, months and years are also used to designate tenses. For example:

"Tahtlum sun ahnkuttie"— ten days (suns) ago.

The comparative degree of adjectives is usually formed by prefixing the word elip (first or foremost) to the adjective:

"Kloshe"— good (positive degree).

"Elip kloshe"— better (comparative degree).

The superlative degree is properly formed by adding the words "kopa konaway" (the total, the whole):

"Elip kloshe kopa konaway"— better than all . . . and better than all, of course, is the best.

Building up a superlative carries us a long way around, but we finally arrive. There is no such thing, as stated earlier, as comparison by inflection . . . but there is still another way to convey the superlative. Adding "delate" (straight, direct) to the comparative gives us the superlative also, because delate itself is superlative:

"Kloshe"— good.

"Elip kloshe"— better.

"Delate elip kloshe"— best; literally, the very better.

In building a superlative, going from good to less good and least good, you would use the word, kimtah (last, afterward):

"Kloshe"— good.

"Kimtah kloshe"— not so good, worse.

"Delate kimtah kloshe"— very worse or worst.

The personal pronouns become possessive by prefixing them to nouns, like "nika nem," my name; "mika kuitan," your horse; "nesika illahee," our land.

Sometimes "s" is added to the personal pronouns in the possessive case; thus, nikas, mine; mikas, yours; nesikas, ours; mesikas, yours; yakas, his or hers; klaskas, theirs. Eells says this mode is used only when the pronoun is the last word in the sentence, thus: "Okoke kuitan nesikas," that horse is ours.

"Nika nanitch yaka"— I see him.

"Yaka kokshut nika"— he hit me.

"Nika klootchman"— my wife or woman.

"Nika tenas man"— my son, little man, boy, or if used by a young woman, may mean my sweetheart.

"Nika tenas klootchman"— my little woman, daughter, girl, sweetheart.

"Nika tumtum"— I think; my thought, guess or opinion.

"Nika tumtum kahkwa"— I agree, I think so, I think like that, I approve.

Among the interrogatives are "Ikta," what? What's up now? etc.

"Kah"— where? whence? whither?

"Kahta"— how? why?

"Kunsih"— how many? how much?

"Klaksta"— who?

"Na" is a general interrogation, and used in many different forms of question.

Numerals are given in their alphabetical order in this dictionary, but we will give them here again in their numerical order and illustrate the manner in which they are used:

"Ikt" —one.	"Sinamokst"— seven.
"Mokst"— two.	"Stotekin"— eight.
"Klone" —three.	"Kwaist"— nine.
"Lakit"— four.	"Tahtlum"— ten.
"Kwinnum"— five.	"Tukamonuk"— one hundred.
"Taghum"— six.	

The Jargon words for eight and nine are but little used, being replaced by the English words or used in combination as: "kwinnum pe klone," five and three for eight, and "kwinnum pe lakit," five and four for nine. Thousands is either represented by the combination "tahtlum tukamonuk," ten hundred, or the English word thousand.

The regularly used combinations of the numerals are quite simple. "Tahtlum pe ikt," eleven, is ten and one; "mokst tahtlum pe kwinnum," twenty-five is literally two tens and five. "Taghum tahtlum" is six tens. "Klone tukamonuk" is three hundred. The year 1926 would be expressed as follows: "Tahtlum tukamonuk (one thousand), kwaist tukamonuk (nine hundred), pe mokst tahtlum pe taghum (and two tens and six)."

The origins of words in the following Chinook-English vocabulary are indicated as follows: Chinook (C); Chehalis (Ch); Clackamas (Cl); Calapooia (Cal); Clallam (Clal); Bellabella (BB); Nootka (N); Klickitat (K); Wasco (W); general Salishan tongues (S); English (E); and Canadian-French (F). Invented words and words of doubtful origin which have been incorporated into the Chinook Jargon are marked (J).

Pronunciation is shown as follows: Accented syllables are indicated by an accent mark ('). This is not invariable in all words, but is occasionally movable. For example, sapolil (bread) is generally accented on the first syllable but occasionally on the last. A general discussion of pronunciation and spelling can be found in Chapter 13, Part One, "Spelling and Pronunciation of Chinook."

CHINOOK-ENGLISH

A

AB'-BA (J): Well, very well.

ACK (J): Nephew.

AD-DE-DAH' (S): Exclamation of pain, sorrow, surprise.

AH'-HA (C): Yes.

AHN'-KUT-TIE or ahnkutte (C): Formerly, in the past, before now, long ago, anciently, ago. (With the accent prolonged on the first syllable, a very long time ago; ancient. The longer the first syllable is held, the longer the time expressed.)
"Hyas ahnkuttie"— very long time ago (literally, much long ago).
"Tenas ahnkuttie"— little while ago.
"Kunsih laly ahnkuttie?"— how long ago?
"Siah ahnkuttie"— very ancient; literally, far ago.
"Ahnkuttie mama"— grandmother.
"Ahnkuttie papa"— grandfather, ancestor, forefather, progenitor.
"Ahnkuttie tillikums"— ancestors, ancient people.
"Ahnkuttie tillikums yiem wawa"— traditions; literally, tales spoken by the ancient people.
"Ahnkuttie laly"— long ago.

A'-KIK or more commonly ik'kik (J): A fishhook.

AL-AH' (J): Expression of surprise.
"Alah, mika chako!"— Oh, here you are!

AL'KI (C): In the future, by and by, after a while, soon, presently, directly, in a little while, hold on, not so fast. (This is the sign of the future tense, shall or will. The days of the week, and the number of weeks, months and years are also used to designate tenses.)
"Nika kumtux alki"— I will understand, I will understand by and by.
"Tenas alki"— in a little while.
"Alki nika klatawa"— I will go presently.
"Iskum dolla, alki pay"— to borrow (get money, pay later).
"Alki nesika klatawa kopa nika boat"— soon we will go in my boat.

AL-LE-KA-CHEEK' (J): Small shell money. This is the small shell also worn as an ornament for the ear (see coop-coop, hykwa.)

AL'-TA or al-tah (C): Now, at the present time.
"Alta yaka chako"— now he comes.
"Nika skookum alta"— I am strong now.
"Waka alta"— not now.

A-MO'-TEH (C): Strawberry (plant or fruit). Occasionally corrupted into almota.

AN-AH! (J): ah! oh! fie!— an exclamation of pain or displeasure.

"Anah, nowitka, mika halo shem!"— Ah, indeed, are you not ashamed!

AN-DI-ALH' (J): A wasp.

A-SHUK' (C): Snow. See snass (cole).

AT-I-MIN' (J): Dead (see memaloose).

ATS (J): A sister, younger than the person speaking of her.

"Elip ats"— older sister. (See kahpho).

"Ats yaka man"— brother-in-law.

"Mama yaka ats"— aunt.

B

BE'-BE (F): A kiss, to kiss or fondle.

BED (E): A bed.

BIT (E): A dime or shilling.

BLOOM (E): A broom.

"Mamook bloom"— to sweep.

BOAT (E): A boat, as distinguished from a canoe; skiff.

"Kopa boat"— aboard.

"Klahanie kopa boat"— overboard.

BOOK (E): A book; volume, pocket-book.

"Tenas book"— a pamphlet.

"Book, yaka mamook kumtux nesika kopa illahee"— a geography.

"Book yaka mamook kumtux nesika kopa lalang"— a grammar.

"Book yaka mamook kumtux nesika kopa nesika"— a physiology.

"Book yaka mamook kumtux nesika kopa stone"— a geology.

"Saghalie Tyee yaka book"— a bible (literally, — God, his book).

BOS'-TON (E): An American, American. (A name derived from the hailing place of the first trading ships to the Pacific.)

"Boston plie"— protestantism.

"Sitkum-siwash-sitkum-Boston"— a half-breed, (half Indian, half American.)

"Boston Illahee"— the United States.

"Mika kumtux Boston wawa?"— do you understand English?

BUR-DASH (F): A hermaphrodite.

BY-BY (E): By-and-by, after a while, sometime hence. (It means a longer time in the future than alki, but like that word is used for shall or will as a sign of future time. With the accent on the first syllable prolonged, it means a very long time hence.)

C

CAL'-I-PEEN (F): A rifle, carbine.

CAM'-AS or kamass, lakamas, camass (N): An edible bulb, a species of hyacinth, which was and still is a principal food of the Indians. It is eaten raw, and is also beaten into a pulp, dried in cakes and eaten in lieu of bread. It is abundant from the Coast Range to the Bitter Root Mountains and was found in abundance in Indian days on the Columbia River flats. It was sometimes called the Siwash onion. The flower is blue, the plant and blossom resembling a hyacinth. In his Nootka Sound Journal (1803-5), John Rodgers Jewitt gives chamass for fruit, also for sweet. However, the preferred spelling has come to be camas.

CA-NIM' (C): A canoe.
"Canim stick"— the cedar or wood from which canoes are usually made.
"Klatawa kopa canim"— to embark, to go in a canoe.
CAP'-A-LA (J): The cheeks.
CA'-PO' (F): A coat.
CHAK'-CHAK (C): The bald eagle.
CHA'-KO or chah'-ko, chahco (N): To come, to approach, to be or become.
(In the latter sense it forms the passive voice in connection with many other words. Often it is joined with adjectives and nouns, and forms other verbs.)
"Nika chako keekwulee"— I am degraded.
"Yaka chako stone"— it is petrified.
"Yaka chako pahtlum"— he is drunk.
Occasionally the passive voice is shown by placing the word iskum before the main word:
"Yaka iskum kow"— he is arrested.
"Nika chako kopa Poteland"— I come from Portland.
"Kloshe mika hyak chako"— good you come quick.
"Chuck chako"— the tide is rising (literally, is coming).
"Chuck chako pe klatawa"— the tides.
"Halo chako"— to linger.
"Wake kunsih yaka chako halo"— indelible, (literally, never will be gone).
"Chako Boston"— to become an American (often said of Indians who are becoming civilized like white people).
"Chako delate till"— to become exhausted.
"Chako elip hiyu"— to exceed.
"Chako halo"— to be destroyed, to disappear, to vanish, to be all gone.
"Chako huloima"— to vary, to become different.
"Chako hyas tumtum"— to become proud.
"Chako kah nika nanitch"— to appear.
"Chako kloshe"— to get well, to become good.
"Chako kloshe tum-tum"— to love, to reform, to become friendly, to get a good heart.
"Chako kunamokst"— to congregate, assemble, convene, meet, unite, join.
"Chako kunamokst nika"— come with me.
"Chako memaloose"— to die, to become rotten, to become decayed (as potatoes or vegetables).
"Chako pahtlum"— to become drunk.

"Chako polaklie"— to become dark, night is coming.
"Chako skookum"— to become strong, especially after a sickness, to show complete recovery.
"Chako solleks"— to become angry, to quarrel.
"Chako pelton"— to become foolish, to be cheated.
"Chako tenas"— to decrease.
"Chako waum tumtum"— to be earnest, to become excited; literally, come warm heart.
"Chako yotl tumtum"— to become glad, to be glad.
CHEE (C): Lately, just now, new, fresh, original, recent.
"Chee nika ko"— I have just arrived.
"Hyas chee"— entirely new, very new.
"Chee chako"— a newcomer, just arrived.
"Delate chee"— entirely new.
"Klootchman yaka chee mallie"— a bride.
CHEE'-CHEE (C): A small bird.
CHESP (J): The neck. (see le-coo).
CHET'-LO (S): An oyster, oysters.
CHET'-WOOT (S): A black bear.
CHIK'-A-MIN (N): Iron, metal, metallic, steel, money, cash, mineral.
"T'kope chikamin"— silver (white metal).
"Pil chikamin"— gold or copper (yellow metal).
"Chikamin lope"— wire, a chain.
"Nika hyas ticky chikamin"— I very much wish money.
"Illahee kah chikamin mitlite"— mines.
"Chikamin piah"— stove.
CHIK'-CHIK or tsik-tsik or tchik-tchik (J): A wagon, cart, wheel, any wheeled vehicle.
"Chik-chik wayhut"— a wagonroad.
"Nika chako kopa chikchik"— I come in a wagon.
"Piah chikchik"— railroad cars.
"Lolo kopa chikchik"— to haul in a wagon.
CHIL'-CHIL or tsil-tsil (C): Buttons, the stars.
CHI-NOOK': A Chinook Indian or the Jargon. The word probably originates from the Chehalis word Tsinuk, their name for the Chinook tribe.
"Chinook canim"— large canoe.
"Chinook illahee"— the land of the Chinook Indians.
"Chinook tillikums"— the Chinook Indians or people.
"Chinook wawa"— the Chinook language. "Mika kumtux Chinook wawa?"— Do you understand the Chinook language?
"Chinook sammon (salmon)"— the quinnat salmon.
"Chinook wind"— a warm, moist, southwest wind of the coastal states of Oregon and Washington, originally so-called by the white settlers at Astoria because it came from the direction of the Chinook camp.
CHITSH (S): A grandmother.
CHOPE (S): A grandfather, (see chitsh).

CHO'-TUB (S): A flea.

CHUCK (N): Water, a river, or stream. Salt chuck — the sea, Skookum chuck—a powerful or rapid stream, Solleks chuck — a rough sea, Chuck chako (killapi) — the tide comes, rises and falls, Saghalie (keekwullee) chuck — high (low) tide.
"Kah mitlite chuck?"— where is the water?
"Muckamuck chuck"— to drink water. "Olo kopa chuck"— thirsty.
"Hyas chuck"— deluge.
"Chuck lapome"— cider.

CHUK'-KIN (S): To kick.

CLY or kely (E): To cry, lament, moan, mourning, weeping (either noun or verb).
"Cly tumtum"— to cry in the heart, to feel sorry, to repent, to mourn, to be full of grief or emotion (deeper in feeling than sick tumtum).

COLE (E): Cold; also a year.
"Hyas cole"— very cold, freezing.
"Cole illahee"— winter, the place or abiding place of cold.
"Cole snass"— hail or snow, frozen rain.
"Cole chuck"— ice; also very cold water, ice water.
"Cole sick"— a cold, ague.
"Cole sick waum sick"— fever and chills, or in the other order, chills and fever.
"Ikt cole"— a year, one winter.
"Tahtlum cole"— ten years or winters.
"Ikt tukamonuk cole"— a hundred winters or years, a century.
"Kah cole chako"— the north; where the cold comes from.
"Kah delate cole mitlite"— the place where the coldest cold abides, the Arctic.

CO'-LEE-CO'-LEE (J): A rat.

COMB (E): A comb.
"Mamook comb illahee"— to harrow.

COOLEY (F): To run, go about, play, walk, travel.
"Cooley kuitan"— a race horse.
"Yahka hyas kumtux cooley"— he knows very well how to run; he can run.
"Cultus cooley"— to saunter, to wander about aimlessly, ramble or stroll.
"Hyak cooley"— to run rapidly or go fast.
"Kopet cooley"— to stop, halt, cease moving.
"Cooley chuck"— river.
(Also signifies a narrow valley, usually dry, through which spring floods run during the melting of the snow. Probably from the French word courir, to run.)

COOP'-COOP (C): Small dentalium, or shell money (see hykwa).

CO'-SHO (F): A pig, pork, ham, bacon.
"Klootchman cosho"— a sow (a pig's woman, to be literal).
"Siwash cosho"— a seal (literally, Indian pig).

"Tenas cosho"— a suckling or small pig.

"Cosho glease"— lard.

"Cosho itlwillie"— hog meat, pork. (From the French, cochon, of the same meaning).

CUL'-TUS or kultus (C): Worthless, good for nothing, without purpose, bad, dissolute, filthy, foul, useless, worn out, damaged beyond repair, and also a degree of worthlessness which cannot be expressed in ordinary English. A cultus siwash is the last word in no-accountness. (A few words are very expressive, meaning so much and expressing that meaning in so much better way than our English words do that they have often been adopted into the English in regions where the Chinook Jargon is used. Cultus is among these words.)

"Cultus man"— a worthless fellow.

"Cultus potlatch"— a present or free gift.

"Cultus he-he"— a joke or jest.

"Cultus nanitch"— to look idly about.

"Cultus mitlite"— to sit idly, or stay where you are, doing nothing.

"Cultus kopa mika"— none of your business.

"Cultus kopa nika"— makes no difference to me; I do not care.

"Delate cultus"— absolute worthlessness, of no manner of use whatever.

D

DA'GO (J): Gnats, "No-see'-ums." (This might have derived from the Indian pronunciation of "they go.")

DE-AUB' (F): The devil, Satan, a demon.

"Deaub yaka illahee"— hell; literally, the devil, his place.

"Spose mika mamook mesachie, deaub iskum mika"— if you do wrong the devil will get you.

DE-LATE' or tlaite (E): Straight, direct, true, truly, exact, definite, definitely, sincere, sincerely, sure, authentic, accurate, very, correctly. (According to James Gilchrist Swan (1857), this word is a corruption of the English word, straight—which seems more likely than the derivation from the French, droite — cited by other authorities.)

"Klatawa delate"— to go straight ahead, the way you are going.

"Delate wawa"— the truth, true talk, a promise, tell the truth, a fact.

"Delate kwinnum cole ahnkuttie"— exactly five years ago.

"Okoke delate"— that is right or it is correct.

"Wake delate"— not right, imperfect.

"Delate nika sick tumtum"— I am very sorry; literally, very I sorry.

"Wawa delate (reversing the phrase delate wawa)"— to speak the truth or speak correctly.

"Delate hyas"— very big indeed, enormous, immense.

"Delate kloshe"— very good.

"Delate hyas kloshe"— very, very good; literally, a big or superlative very good; also an equivalent of majestic, magnificent, awe-inspiring.

"Delate kumtux"— to know for a certainty, sure, to prove.

"Delate pahtl"— full to the brim, chockfull.

"Delate sick tumtum"— very sad, very sorry, grief, sad at heart.

"Delate tenas sun"— dawn, the very beginning of the morning, daybreak.

"Delate yaka illahee"— a native of the country; literally, his very home.

"Delate yaka kumtux"— an expert; literally, perfectly he knows.

"Delate nika wawa"— I am speaking the truth; literally, truth I say.

"Delate tenas"— just a little.

D'LY (E): Dry, dryness, arid, without water. (An Indian attempt to pronounce the English word dry.)

"Chako d'ly"— to become dry.

"Mamook d'ly"— to dry up, to make dry.

"D'ly tupso"— hay; literally, dry grass.

DOC'-TIN (E): Doctor, physician, surgeon, healer. The word as used referred to a white doctor. If an Indian doctor was meant the term became Siwash doctin.

"Nika ticky doctin"— I want the doctor.

"Dockin kopa letah"— doctor of the teeth.

"Doctin kopa seeowist or seahost"— doctor of the eyes or face.

DOLLA (E): A dollar, money. (An Indian attempt to use the English word dollar; sometimes pronounced tollah).

"Chickamin dolla"— a silver dollar.

"Pil dolla"— gold coin. (Pil refers to the color. Pil chickamin is copper money or coins.)

"Sitkum dolla"— half a dollar.

"Ikt dolla"— one dollar.

"Tahtlum dolla"— ten dollars.

"Dolla seeowist"— spectacles (eyes one pays for).

DUTCHMAN: Any white man other than an American, a Frenchman or an Englishman.

E

EE'-NA (C): A beaver.

"Eena stick"— willow (beaverwood).

EK-KAH'-NAM (C): A tale or story.

EK'-KEH (C): A brother-in-law.

EK-KO-LI (C): A whale.

E-KONE' (J): The Good Spirit.

EK-SKAUN (C): Wood, wooden.

E-KU'-TOCH (J): The Bad Spirit.

E-LA-HAN, or E-lan (S): Aid, assistance, alms.

"Mamook elan"— to help, to give alms or assistance.

E-LAK'-HA (J): The sea otter.

E'-LIP (S): First, before, beginning, ahead, prior, senior, elder, original. (For the use of elip in the formation of the positive, comparative and superlative degrees of adjectives, see the introduction to this section of the book.)

E-LI'-TEE (J): A slave.

E-MEEK' (J): The back.

E-MEETS' (J): The nose.

E-MI'-H (J): The breast, the chest.

E-MIN'-TE-PU (J): The muskrat.

EN'-A-TI (C): Across, beyond, opposite to, on the other side of.
"Nika ticky klatawa enati kopa chuck"— I want to go across the water.
"Yaka mitlite enati kopa city"— he lives opposite to the city; or literally, across from the city.

E-QUAN'-NAT (C): Salmon. This word is the original of Quinnat, a specific name for the Chinook or king salmon. (see Sammon).

E-SALT'-H or ye-salt'-h (W): Indian corn, maize.

ES'-SAL (C): To come.

E-TAM'-A-NA (S): A prophet.

ETH'-LAN or it-lan (C): A fathom.

E'-TIN-WILL (S): The ribs.

ET'-SHUM (C): The heart.

ET-SIT'-SA (S): Sick.

G

GET-UP' or ket-op' (E): To get up, rise, risen. (It is difficult for Indians to get exact English sounds, so they often pronounce this word as if it were spelled ket-op.)

GLEASE (E): Grease. This was another attempt to pronounce English. Indians converted the r into l, and grease became glease.
"Hiyu glease"— very fat.
"Tatoosh glease"— butter. (Tatoosh means breasts, milk, udder.)
"Glease mitlite kopa bone"— marrow.
"Glease piah"— a candle.

GOOM or la-goom (F): Pitch; resin.

GOOM STICK: Pine, fir or spruce.

H

HAH'-LAKL (C): Wide, open.
"Mamook hahlakl la pote"— open the door.
"Chako hahlakl"— expression used when applied to thin spaces in the forest. It could be translated literally as "coming open."
"Mamook hahlakl"— to open or to make open.

HAHT-HAHT (S): The mallard duck.

HAK'-AT-SHUM (E): Handkerchief (An Indian imitation of the English word handkerchief).

HA-LET' (S): To tremble.

HALO (J): No, none, without, all gone, not. (see wake)
"Halo chickamin nika"— I have no money.
"Halo pish chako"— no fish come.
"Halo glease"— without fat, lean.
"Halo iktas"— no goods, destitute.
"Yaka wind halo chako"— literally, his breath does not come; dead.
HAS'-LITCH (J): Liver.
HAUL (E): Haul, to pull or draw.
"Mamook haul"— must haul.
HE-HE (C):Laugh, laughter, mirth, fun, to laugh, glee, sport, a game, ridicule. He-he may be used as noun, verb, or adjective.
"Cultus hehe"— a joke.
"Mamook hehe"— to laugh.
"Wake hehe"— serious, not to laugh.
"Kloshe hehe"— a good game.
"Hehe house"— an amusement place, a dance house, a play house.
"Hehe tumtum"— a jolly spirit, good natured.
HELP (E): Help, aid, assist, assistance. (This may be used as noun or verb. Used as a verb it is usually preceded by mamook and sometimes by potlatch — makes help in the one case; gives help in the other.)
HI-YU' (N): Much, plenty, abundance. (Used with reference to quantity and numbers rather than size or degree.)
"Hiyu tillikum"— a crowd.
"Hiyu muckamuck"— plenty of food.
"Tenas hiyu"— a small number.
"Wake hiyu"— not many, very few.
"Kopet hiyu"— enough.
"Hiyu wawa"— much talk, a clamor.
"Hiyu tillikums kopa house"— an audience; many people in house.
HOH-HOH (J): To cough.
HO-KU-MELH (S): To gather; glean.
HOOL-HOOL (C): Mouse.
HOUSE (E): House.
"Siwash house"— Indian house.
"Mahkook house"— a store or trading house, a shop.
"Skookum house"— a jail, literally a strong house.
"Muckamuck house"— hotel, restaurant or any eating place.
HOW (J): Listen; attend.
HOWH (J): Turn to, or get to work briskly, hurry.
HOW-KWUTL (J): Expresses inability. How could? Cannot.
"How-kwutl klap yahka?"— how could I find her?
HUL-LEL' (C): To shake or tremble. (Used with the verb mamook, it becomes active. Mamook hullel means to make shake or tremble.)
HUL-O'-I-MA (C): Other, another, different, difference, averse, diverse, foreign, odd, strange, queer, unusual, separate.
"Huloima tillikum"— a different tribe of people.

"Klatawa kopa huloima illahee"— to go to another place or country or abiding place, to emigrate.

"Huloima mamook"— miracle.

"Hyas huloima"— a big difference.

"Huloima tumtum"— to dissent or disagree, a difference of opinion.

"Huloima wawa"— a different language, a foreign tongue; also to mispronounce or say the word wrong.

HUMM (J): To smell, stink; stench, an odor; putrid.

"Humm opoots"— stinking tail, hence used to denote skunk.

"Yaka humm"— it smells.

"Hyas humm"— a very bad smell.

"Mamook humm"— to smell.

"Kloshe humm"— a pleasant smell.

"Humm itlwillie"— carrion.

HUNL'-KIH (C): Curled, curly, crooked, knotted.

HUY-HUY (J): A bargain or exchange, to barter or trade. This was originally mahkook, that being the Nootkan for buy, sell or trade, there being no distinction, as barter was the first order of prehistoric trade. Then mahsh (F. marchand) was introduced by the French, but as the distinction between buying, selling and exchanging required more definite terms, mahkook came to apply to buying, mahsh to selling, and huyhuy to exchange.

"Huyhuy la sell"— to change the saddle.

"Huyhuy tumtum"— to change one's mind. It is said to mean a hasty exchange in some cases, and that it got its origin in the French for yes, yes — oui, oui.

"Mamook huyhuy"— to change, to trade.

"Nika ticky huyhuy kuitan kopa canim"— I want to trade horse for canoe.

"Mika ticky huyhuy kuitan kopa canim?"— do you want to trade horse for canoe?

HWAH! (J): Ah, indeed! Exclamation of surprise.

HY-AK' (C): Quick, hurry, swift, fast, quickly, rapidly, sudden, suddenly, rapidity of motion.

"Mamook hyak"— to make haste, to be prompt.

"Hyak yaka chako"— quickly he comes.

"Wake hyak"— slow, not fast.

HY-AS' (N): Large, great, very, wide, big, vast, when applied to size; can be used for very, arduous, celebrated, etc.

"Hyas tyee"— a great chief.

"Hyas ahnkuttie"— a very long time ago.

"Hyas Sunday"— a holiday like Christmas or Fourth of July.

"Hyas tenas"— very small.

"Hyas kloshe"— very good.

"Okoke house yaka hyas"— that house, it is large.

"Nika hyas ticky klatawa"— I very much want to go.

"Hyas tick-tick"— clock.

"Hyas house"— mansion.

HY'-KWA (hiaqua, hiagua, haiqua, ioqua) (N): Shell money or wampum, large dentalium — one of the tooth shells.

This formerly was used as money among Northwestern Indians. The kind prized most highly was the dentalium pretiosum, a long, white, quill-like shell, procured in deep water from the coasts of the straits and inland seas by thrusting a mass of blubber attached to a long pole down upon the shells, which grew point up on the rocks, and thus detaching them. It was strung upon thin deer sinew about a fathom in length. A smaller kind of the same shell was also used as money and called coop-coop or allekacheek. These shells were sometimes worn as ornaments in pierced ears and noses.

The tooth shell is extremely long and slender. It is shaped like an elephant's tusk, is two to three inches in length and one-sixteenth to one-eighth inch in diameter. The shell is a hollow, slightly curved white tube with fine rings and striations on the surface. There is a hole at each end through which the sinew is run and the shell is of slightly greater diameter at one end than at the other.

I

IK-HOL' (C): River, stream (see cooley).

IK'-IK (C): Fishhook.

IK-POO'-IE (C): To shut, close, stop by closing; to cork.

"Ikpooie la pote"— shut the door.

"Mamook ikpooie"— to surround; to shut.

"Ikpooie kwolan"— deaf; a closed ear.

IKT (C): The numeral one; once, a unit or single thing; also the indefinite articles, a and an.

"Ikt man"— a man, one man.

"Ikt dolla"— one dollar.

"Ikt cole"— one year.

"Ikt-ikt-man"— some one or other.

"Ikt nika klatawa kopa yaka house"— once I go to his house.

"Ikt tahlkie"— day before yesterday.

"Ikt time ikt moon"— the time one month.

"Ikt time kopa klone moon"— the time of three moons; three months; quarterly.

"Kopet ikt"— to stop alone, solitary, singly, only one.

IK'-TA (C): What? (interrogative pronoun). There are three of these: Klaksta, who? Ikta or kahta, what? Kunsih, how many or how much? Also, when? How much time or how many days?

"Ikta okoke?"— what is that?

"Ikta mika ticky?"— what do you want?

"Ikta mamook?"— what's the matter? what's doing?

"Ikta mika mamook?"— what are you doing?

IK'-TAS (C): Things, garments, dress, clothes, goods, merchandise, utensils — almost any personal possession.

The use of the same word for what (ikta) and for things (iktas) is found in other Coast Indian dialects. Iktas is a very expressive word and was long ago adopted into the English spoken by the early settlers.

"Kah mika iktas?"— where are your things?

"Halo iktas mitlite"— there is nothing here.

"Nika hiyu iktas"— I have many things or goods.

IL'-LA-HEE (C): Country, land, earth, region, district, soil, farm, field, ranch, the place where one resides, home.

"Boston Illahee"— United States.

"King George (Chauch) Illahee"— England.

"Passaiooks Illahee"— France.

All other whites came from Dutchman Illahee, or Dutchman yaka illahee, as they commonly expressed it.

"Siwash illahee"— Indian country and later an Indian reservation.

"Saghalie Illahee"— heaven.

"Keekwullie Illahee"— hell. (Saghalie means above and keekwullie below.)

"Okoke illahee yaka hyas kloshe"— this land is very good.

"Delate yaka illahee"— one's native land.

"Konaway okoke illahee"— the world; literally, all this country, everything, everywhere.

"Konaway illahee konaway kah"— all places all where — the universe.

"Saghalie Tyee yaka Illahee"— God, His Country, Heaven.

"Kah mika illahee?"— where is your country? where do you come from?

"Kloshe illahee"— garden.

IN'-A-POO (C): A louse.

"Sopena inapoo"— a louse that jumps; a flea.

IN'-A-TI or enati (C): Across.

"Inati chuck"— over the river.

IP'-SOOT (C): To hide, to keep secret, to conceal; hidden, sly, concealed; to hide one's self; to hide anything.

"Ipsoot wawa"— to whisper.

"Ipsoot klatawa"— to slip away secretly.

IS'-ICK (C): A paddle, an oar.

"Mamook isick"— to paddle, to row.

"Isick stick"— any wood from which an oar or paddle is made—alder, ash (literally, paddlewood).

IS'-KUM (C): Get, hold, receive, accept, secure, nab, catch, recover, obtain; seize; to take hold of, amass.

"Iskum okoke lope"— hold on to that rope.

"Mika na iskum?"— did you get it?

"Mika iskum?"— you get?

"Iskum piah stick"— get some firewood.

"Iskum klootchman"— get a woman; get married.
"Iskum kumtux"— get understanding, to learn.
"Iskum kopa tumtum"— to believe.
"Potlatch nika?"— give me?
"Iskum"— take it.
"Kah mika iskum?"— where did you get it?
"Nika iskum kopa stick?"— I got it in the woods.
"Iskum sapolil"— harvest.

IT'-LAN or eth'-lan (C): A fathom, the length of the arms extended.

IT'-LO-KUM (C): A gambling game, the game of "hand," a common amusement among all the tribes.
"Mamook itlokum"— to gamble.

ITL'-WIL-LIE (C): Meat, flesh, muscle of a person or animal.
"Lemooto itlwillie, or lemooto yaka itlwillie"— mutton; literally, sheep, his meat.
"Moosmoos yaka itlwillie"— beef; cow, its meat.
"Mowitch yaka itlwillie"— deer, its flesh; venison.
"Tenas moosmoos yaka itlwillie"— veal; little cow, its flesh.
"Konaway nika itlwillie sick"— all my muscles are sore.

ITS'-WOOT (C): A bear, a black bear.
"Itswoot pasese"— a dark, thick cloth, a dark blanket. Probably originally used by Indians who saw a resemblance between the heavy dark blankets of the Hudson's Bay Company and the fur of a black bear.

K

KAH? (C): Where? whence? whither?
"Kah mika klatawa?"— where are you going?
"Halo kah"— nowhere.
"Konaway kah"— everywhere; literally, all where.
"Kah mika mitlite?"— where do you live or stay?
"Kah mika illahee?"— where is your land or where is your country?
"Kah mika chaco?"— where do you come from?
"Kah yaka sick?"— where is he sick? what is the matter?
"Kah cole chaco"— where the cold comes from — north.
"Kah sun chaco"— where the sun rises or comes from — east.
"Kah sun klatawa"— where the sun goes — west.
"Kah sun mitlite kopa sitkum sun"— where the sun is at half sun — mid-day — south.

KAH-DE'-NA (C): To fight.
"Clatsop tillikum kadeena Chehalis"— the Clatsops fight with the Chehalis.

KAH'-KAH (J): A crow.

KAH'-KWA (N): Like, similar to, equal with, alike, as so, as also, even as, thus, such, hence, because, inasmuch; mostly used for like and alike.
"Kahkwa tyee"— like a chief, aristocratic, kingly.
"Kahkwa nika tumtum"— like as my heart; as I think; so I think.

"Kahkwa hyas nika"— as large as I am; as big I.

"Halo kahkwa"— not like, unlike.

"Kahkwa spose"— as if; like supposed.

"Yaka kahkwa"— alike; it like.

"Kopet kahkwa"— that is all.

"Delate kahkwa'— exactly the same.

"Kloshe kahkwa"— that is right; good so; so be it; amen. (The Lord's
     Prayer in the Chinook jargon ends with the expression: "kloshe
     kahkwa."

According to Myron Eells (1843-1907), who lived among the Puget Sound
Indians practically all his life, "kahkwa" is often used with other words,
especially nouns, changing them into adverbs and sometimes into adjectives.
The following phrases illustrate what he means:

"Kahkwa chikamin"— metallic; like metal.

"Kahkwa cole illahee"— wintry; like the country of the cold.

"Kahkwa chuck"— fluid; liquid, like water.

"Kahkwa tillikum"— friendly.

KAH-LO'-KEN (C): A swan.

KAH'-MOOKS or Komooks (C): A dog. (Pronounced differently in different
     localities. Among the Kwakiutl it is comox. Comox, a coal mining town
     on Vancouver Island in the original Kwakiutl country, takes its name from
     the word.)

"Kahkwa kahmooks"— like a dog, beastly.

"Kahmooks house"— dog house.

"Kahmooks wawa"— bark of a dog.

KAH'-NA-WAY (C): Acorn or acorns.

"Kahnaway stick"— the oak.

KAH'-TA (C): How? why?

"Kahta mika mamook okoke?"— why (do) you do that?

"Kahta mika chaco?"— how (did) you come?

"Kahta mika?"— how (are) you?

"Pe kahta?"— and why? what for?

"Kahta kopa yaka?"— how is he?

KA-LAK'-A-LA or Kulakula (C): A bird, a fowl, a winged insect, a wing.
     (It is said to be an imitation of the notes of a wild goose when flying —
     hence flying bird.)

"Kalakala house"— a nest.

KAL-A-KWAH'-TEE (J): The silky inner bark of the cedar. This bark,
     stripped in long filaments and made fast to a cord or sinew in a long fringe,
     was worn by Chinook and other Indian women of the lower country for
     skirts and capes. The word also means petticoat. Chinese and Japanese
     make similar garments of long grass.

KA-LI'-TAN (C): An arrow, a shot, a bullet.

"Kalitan le sac"— a quiver for arrows, originally; but when guns were
     introduced the expression also meant a shotpouch, and also was used
     for bullets and lead.

KAMAS: See Camas.

KA'MO'-SUK (C): Beads.

"Tyee kamosuk"— the large blue beads so highly prized in the fur-trading days.

KAP-SWOL'-LA (J): To steal, rob; a theft, larceny; a thief.

"Yaka kapswolla canim"— he stole the canoe.

"Kuitan kapswolla"— horse thief.

"Mika kapswolla okoke?"— did you steal that?

"Kapswolla klootchman"— steal a woman; rape.

"Yaka kumtux kapswolla"— he knows how to steal.

"Yaka kapswolla man"— he is a thief.

Used with other words "kapswolla" acquires a larger significance than in any of the examples given above:

"Kapswolla klatawa"— to go secretly, or steal away.

"Kapswolla mamook"— to do secretly.

"Wake kloshe mika kapswolla"— (not good you steal). Thou shalt not steal.— Commandment.

"Kapswolla wawa"— to speak ill.

"Kapswolla moosum"— literally "steal sleep." (Used to mean adultery, illicit sexual intercourse.)

"Kapswolla kopa klootchman"— to elope.

KAT'-SUK (C): The middle or center.

KAUP'-HO (C): An elder brother or cousin. Also "elip ow," but "kimtah ow," younger brother.

KAU'-PY (J): Coffee (An Indian attempt to pronounce the word in English.)

KA-WAK' (S): To fly.

KAW'-KA-WAK (C): Yellow or pale green.

KEE'-KWUL-LIE (C): Low, below, under, beneath, down, inward.

"Mamook keekwullie"— to lower.

"Mitlite keekwullie"— to set down, put under, place beneath.

"Keekwullie"— low.

"Elip keekwullie"— lower.

"Elip keekwullie kopa konaway"— lower than all or lowest.

"Klatawa keekwullie kopa chuck"— to dive; literally, to go beneath the water.

"Mahsh keekwullie kopa illahee"— to bury; to put under the ground.

KEEL'-AL-LY (C): A medicine man.

KEEP'-WOT (C): Needle; pin; thorn; sting of an insect.

KEH-LO'-KE or kaloke (C): A swan.

KEH'-SU or kisu (C): An apron.

KEH'-WA (J): Because (see kahkwa).

"Kehwa yaka memaloose"— because she (or he, or it) is dead.

KE'-LOK (C): Crane.

KES'-CHI (C): Notwithstanding; although.

"Keschi mika wawa wake mamook"— although he said not to do it.

KET'-LING (E): Kettle, can, basin.

KET'-WIL-LA (C): Cellar, pit.

KIL-IT'-SUT (C): Flint, bottle, glass.

KILL'-A-PI or keellapi (C): To turn, return, overturn, upset, reverse, retreat, capsize, and often to denote crooked or twisted deformities.

"Killapi canim"— to upset a canoe.

"Hyak killapi"— to return quickly, to hurry back.

"Killapi kopa house"— go back to the house.

"Mika killapi alta?"— have you returned now?

"Mamook killapi"— to bring back or to send back.

"Killapi tumtum"— to change your mind, reverse your opinion.

"Killapi seeowist"— crossed or crooked eyes.

"Killapi teahwit"— crooked legs or arms.

KIM'-TAH (C): Behind, after, afterwards, last, since, back, rear, subsequent, younger.

"Klatawa kimtah"— to go behind, to follow.

"Delate kimtah"— last.

"Nika elip, pe yaka kimtah"— I first and he afterwards.

"Okoke kimtah"— the one behind.

"Kimtah nika nanitch mika"— since I saw you.

"Kimtah sitkum sun"— afternoon.

"Kimtah kloshe"— worse.

KING CHAUTSH (E): A King George man. (Another Indian attempt to pronounce an English word.)

KIN'-NI-KIN-NIK (C): Smoking weed. (Originally a prepared mixture but later referred to certain plants.)

Coastal Indians smoked the leaves of the Kinnikinnik or bear-berry (Arctostaphylos uva-ursi)— a pretty, trailing shrub with reddish bark and evergreen leaves. The fruit is a bright red berry which was eaten by both Indians and bears.

KI'-NOOTL (C): Tobacco; smoking.

KISH'-KISH (C): To drive as to drive horses or cattle.

"Mamook kishkish"— to drive or impel, make drive.

"Yaka kishkish nika"— he drove me away.

"Mamook kishkish okoke moosmoos"— drive away that ox or cow.

KIS'-SU or kehsu (C): An apron.

KI'-WA (W): Crooked.

KI'-YA (S): Entrails, bowels.

KLAH (C): Free or clear from, in sight; to escape.

"Alta yaka klah"— now he is in sight.

"Klataka klah"— to escape and get away, as a prisoner escaping.

"Yaka klatawa klah"— he escaped.

"Chako klah"— to come up, as seed; to clear up, if used in speaking of the weather; to open out, meaning open spaces in the woods.

"Mamook klah"— to uncover.

KLA'-HA-NIE (C): Out of doors, outside, out, without, exterior.

"Mamook klahanie okoke"— put that out.

"Chako klahanie"— to emerge or come out from, to be delivered.
"Klatawa klahanie"— to go out.
"Mahsh klahanie"— to throw out or eject.
"Klahanie kopa house"— out of doors, out of the house.
"Klatawa nesika klahanie kopa town"— let us go away from the city.
KLA-HOW'-YA? (C): How do you do? good day, good morning, good
evening, or good-by (the ordinary salutation whether meeting or parting).
"Klahowya sikhs"— good day, friend; good-bye, friend; how are you,
friend?
KLA-HOW'-YUM (C): Poor, wretched, miserable, needy, in distress, com-
passion.
"Mamook klahowyum"— to give alms; to take pity.
"Hyas klahowyum nesika"— we are very poor.
KLAK (C): Off, out, away; to take off.
"Klak kopa ooahut"— get out of the road.
"Mamook klak capo"— take off the coat.
"Klak kwolan"— to clip off the ears.
KLAK'-STA (C): Who? whose? which? which one? any.
"Klaksta okoke Boston man?"— who is that American?
"Klaksta yahwa?"— who is there?
"Halo klaksta"— no one, not any.
"Klaksta mamook okoke?"— who did that?
"Ikt man, klonas klaksta"— a man, I don't know whom, therefore some-
body.
"Konaway klaksta"— everyone.
KLAK'-WUN (S): To wipe or lick.
"Klakwun la-tahb"— wipe off the table.
KLALE (C): Black or dark blue, also green; ignorant.
"Okoke pasese yaka klale"— that blanket it is black.
"Klale nika tumtum"— ignorant is my mind.
"Sitkum-klale"— brown; half black.
KLAP (C): To find, arrive.
"Nika klap kopa polaklie"— I arrived at night.
"Mika klap mika canim?"— did you find your canoe?
"Tenas klap"— to be with child, "tenas," little, always standing for child
when used in that manner.
"Klap wawa"— to learn a language.
"Klap tumtum"— to decide or arrive at an opinion.
KLA'-PITE (C): Thread, twine.
KLA-POO'-CHUS (C): Beard (see tupso).
KLAS'-KA (C): They, thine, them, their, theirs, others (anything pertaining
to the third person, plural number).
"Klaska klatawa kopa Clallam illahee"— they go (or went) to the Clallam
country.
"Nika nanitch klaska"— I see them.
"Okoke klaska illahee"— this is their land.

KLAT'-A-WA (N): To go, flee, travel, move away, migrate, start, leave, begone, get out, depart.
"Klatawa teahwhit"— to go on foot, to walk.
"Yaka klatawa kopa Seattle"— he goes, or he went, to Seattle.
"Mamook klatawa"— to make go or send.
KLA'-WAH (C): Slow, slowly, tardily; lazy.
"Klatawa klawah"— go slowly.
"Yahka chaco klawah"— he comes slowly.
"Wawa klawah"— speak slowly.
KLA'-WHOP (C): A hole, pit, cellar.
KLEM'-A-HUN (S): To stab, wound, spear.
KLIK'-A-MUKS (C): Blackberries; dewberries.
KLIK'-WAL-LIE (C): Brass, brass armlet, brass wire.
KLILE (C): Sour; bitter.
KLIM-IN'-A-WHIT (C): A lie, falsehood; to lie; untrue.
"Hyas kumtux kliminawhit"— he is a big liar.
"Yaka kwonesum kliminawhit"— he always lies.
KLIM'-MIN (C): Soft, not hard, fine in substance, fine.
"Klimmin sapolil"— flour, grain ground fine.
"Chako klimmin"— to become soft, melt.
"Klimmin illahee"— soft or marshy ground, mud.
"Wake klimmin or halo klimmin"— not soft, hard.
"Mamook klimmin"— to make become soft or to soften by working, as dressing a deerskin until it is pliable as cloth.
KLIP or klep (C): Deep, sunken; to sink.
"Klip chuck"— deep water.
"Klip sun"— sunset; literally, sinks sun.
KLIS'-KWISS (C): A mat made of cattail rushes.
"Kliskwiss yaka kloshe kopa bed"— the mat is good for a bed.
KLOH-KLOH (C): Oyster or oysters (see chetlo).
KLO'-NAS (C): Perhaps, doubtful, might, may, I do not know, maybe so, who knows? (An expression of uncertainty or doubt; the Jargon equivalent for the Spanish term, quien sabe.)
"Klonas?"— who knows?
"Klonas nika klatawa"— perhaps, or maybe, I go.
"Kah mika kahpho?"— where is your brother?
"Klonas"— I do not know.
"Mika tumtum hiyu snass okoke sun?"— do you think it will rain much today?
"Klonas"— I don't know.
"Klonas yaka chaco tomollo"— perhaps he will come tomorrow.
KLONE (C): Three (the numeral).
"Klone tillikum"— three people.
"Klone sun"— three days.
"Klone canim"— three canoes.

KLOOK (E): Crooked (see killapi).

"Klook teahwit"— lame, crooked legs or arms.

KLOOTCH'-MAN (N): A woman, a female of any animal; a wife.

"Tenas klootchman"— a little woman, a girl or maiden.

"Kah mika klootchman?"— where is your wife?

"Klootchman kuitan"— a mare.

"Tenas yaka tenas klootchman"— a granddaughter, daughter of daughter.

"Klootchman yaka mama"— mother-in-law; woman, her mother.

"Klootchman yaka ats"— sister-in-law; woman, her sister.

KLO-SHE (N): Good.

John Meares was first to record the word, which he spelled "cloosh." Callicum used it on Meares' ship in 1788. It has no definite origin, but seems to come from the similarity of several tribal words and is evidently early Jargon. Its most general use is as the equivalent of the adjective, good. The Nootkan is "klohtl" and so is the Tokwhat; in Makah, an isolated Nootkan tribe, it is "klotelo" and in Nisqually, the word is "klob." Shaw gives forty-five meanings such as good, well, well enough, affable, amiable, apt, auspicious, beautiful, beloved, beneficial, convenient, efficient, elegant, even, fair, fine, fortune, fragrant, gay, graceful, hospitable, meek, intimate, kind, mild, modest, moral, neat, nice, pleasant, plain, please, practical, pretty, right, reliable, safe, respectable, secure, still, smooth, splendid, useful, upright, virtuous, untarnished. Their exact meanings can be determined only by the words used with and the sense used in, for even the forty-five may be extended, as may be seen in some of the examples given.

"Kloshe nanitch"— look good, look well, look out, look sharp, take care, guard, defend, nurse, watch, provide.

"Delate hyas kloshe"— magnificent; literally, perfectly very good.

"Elip kloshe"— better.

"Elip kloshe kopa konaway"— best; literally better than all.

"Mamook kloshe"— make good or pleasing, adorn, decorate, arrange, fix, behave, cure, prepare, repair.

"Wake kloshe"— not good, not well, unkind, unfavorable, wrong.

"Wake kloshe kopa mahkook"— not good to sell, unsalable.

"Kloshe kopa mahkook"— good to sell, salable, merchantable.

"Kloshe kopa nika"— I am satisfied; good enough for me.

"Kloshe kopa cultus potlatch"— liberal, generous, good about giving.

"Kloshe kopet"— be still.

"Kloshe mitlite"— remain, hold on.

"Kloshe tumtum"— love, delight, well meaning, good intention, happy, favorable, friendly.

"Kloshe chako"— all right, come on, come good.

'Kloshe kahkwa"— well, very well, so be it, enough, amen.

"Kloshe tumtum mika chako"— this is a form of invitation signifying welcome, literally, good intentions you come.

KLOSHE-SPOSE (N & E): a combination of good and suppose. Shall or may I, let me, good if—or their equivalent.

"Kloshe-spose nika klatawa?"— shall I or may I go?

"Kloshe-spose nika mamook pia okoke?"— shall I cook that?

KLUH or **klugh** (C): To tear; to plow.

KLUK-ULH' (C): Broad, or wide, as of a plank.

KO (C): To reach, to arrive at.

"Chee klaska ko"— now they arrive, or they have just come.

"Kunsih nesika ko kopa Nisqually?"— when shall we arrive at Nisqually?

"Tahlkie sun nika ko kopa Olympia."— yesterday I arrived at Olympia.

KO'-KO: To knock.

KO'-KO-STICK (J): Woodpecker (knock-tree).

KOK'-SHUT (N): To break, beat, hit, bruise, burst, cleave, hurt, knock, rap, tear, slap, shatter, split; also broken, demolished, torn, bruised; a break. (Mamook is often used with it to make it passive.)

"Nika kokshut yaka, or nika mamook kokshut yaka"— I hit him (both would be proper).

"Nika kokshut or chako kokshut"— I am hurt (both would be proper).

"Hyas kokshut"— much broken.

"Hiya kokshut"— many broken, many pieces, all broken to pieces. (Another way of showing the active and passive.)

"Chako kokshut"— broken.

"Mamook kokshut"— to break. (Mamook is work, the act of doing things.)

KON'-A-WAY (C): All, every, total, universal, entire, aggregate, the sum, the whole.

"Klaska konaway klatawa"— they have all gone.

"Konaway tillikum"— everybody, all the people everywhere.

"Konaway ikta"— everything.

"Konaway kah"— everywhere.

"Konaway sun"— every day.

KOO'-SAH (C): Sky, heaven.

KO'-PA (C): According to, around, about, concerning, to, in, into, unto, with, towards, of, there, in that place, than for, from, on, during, through, instead of. Kopa is the principal preposition in the Jargon.

There are nine words and three phrases which are used as prepositions, but "kopa" is used more than all the others. "Kunamokst" is sometimes used for "with," "kopa saghalie" (pronounced like sockalee) for "over" and "keekwullie" for "under." Kopa has such a variety of meanings that its significance in each case can be known only by the connection in which it is used. Some of these are exact opposites, like "from" and "to."

"Yaka chako kopa saghalie"— he came from heaven (above).

"Yaka klatawa kopa saghalie"— he went to heaven.

"Alta nika potlatch wawa kopa mika kopa okoke pepah"— now I give talk to you about this picture (or paper).

"Yaka mitlite kopa chuck"— he is on the water.

"Yaka mitlite kopa canim"— he is in the canoe.

"Yaka klatawa kopa stick"— he has gone into the woods.

"Kopa ikt moon yaka mitlite yukwa"— during one month he will stay here.

"Kopa yaka wawa John yaka memaloose"— according to his talk John (he) is dead.

"Saghalie kopa mountain"— on top of the mountain.

"Jesus yaka memaloose kopa nesika"— Jesus he died for us, or instead of us.

Kopa is often prefixed to a noun to show the possessive case: "Okoke kuitan kopa John"— this horse is John's (belongs to).

As an adverb: "Yaka kamooks kopa"— his dogs are there. Used thus the last syllable is accented and prolonged — ko-pa-a.

The commonly used word for "there" is "yahwa": "Nika kuitan elip kloshe kopa yaka kuitan"— my horse is better than his horse. "Kopa nika house"— at my house, or in my house. "Lolo okoke kopa mika"— take that with you. "Cultus kopa nika"— it is nothing to me.

KO'-PET (C): Stop, quit, leave off, enough, only, alone, except, enough, submit, that is all.

"Kopet wawa"— stop talking.

"Kopet hiyu"— enough, plenty.

"Kloshe kopet"— be still.

"Kopet ikt"— only one, each, alone, lonely.

"Kopet okoke"— enough of that, that's all.

"Kopet ikt time"— once.

"Kopet kumtux"— to stop knowing, to forget.

"Kopet nika mitlite"— only I remain, or am in this place.

"Wake siah kopet"— nearly finished, not far from enough.

"Mamook kopet"— make stop or to finish, fulfill, complete, quench, conclude.

"Mamook pia kopet"— make the fire quit, go out, put out the fire, quench it.

"Kopet tomollo"— day after tomorrow.

"Kopet cooley"— to halt, to stop walking, moving or running.

"Konaway klatawa kopet yaka"— all went except him.

"Halo kopet"— incomplete. ("Wake yaka kopet" is used also for incomplete or unfinished, meaning literally, not it is stop.)

"Wawa kloshe kopet"— to forbid.

"Kopet alta"— finished now.

KOW (C): To tie, to fasten, to be fastened.

"Kow mika kuitan"— tie your horse.

"Mika mamook kow mika kuitan?"— have you tied your horse?

"Nowitka, yaka kow"— yes, he is tied.

"Ikt kow"— a bundle, a parcel, a package, a pack. (Ikt is one and the pack, parcel or bundle was tied around with straps, strings or rope.)

"Mamook kow"— to tie, hitch or shackle; to make it tied up.

"Mahsh kow"— to untie (mahsh, here, meaning release).

KU'-I-TAN (C): Horse.

"Klatawa kopa kuitan"— to ride; go on a horse.

"Yaka hyas kloshe kuitan?"— is that a good horse?

"Cooley kuitan"— a race horse.

"Stone kuitan"— a stallion.

"Kuitan lepee"— hoofs.

KULL (C): Hard in substance, solid, tough, difficult.

"Chako kull"— to become hard.

"Halo kull" or "wake kull"— not hard, soft, tender, easy.

"Kull stick"— any hard wood, usually oak, as it is the only hardwood of the Northwest.

"Mamook kull"— to make become hard, to cause to harden.

"Kull snass"— hard rain, therefore snow, hail, ice.

"Kull tatoosh"— cheese.

KUL'-LAH (S): A fence, a rail, a pen, an enclosure, a corral.

"Kullah stick"— fence rails.

Kullah is said originally to have meant the stockade within which the Indian houses were built for protection. As it is Salish this is probably true. The Salish were flatheads, and the longheads of the far north were from time immemorial the ancient and hereditary enemies of the flatheads or Salish tribes. Those stockades surrounding Siwash villages were a familiar sight long after they no longer served their original use.

KUM'-TUX or kumtucks (N): Know, learn, be acquainted with, knowledge, wisdom, sense, recognize, believe, understand.

"Mika kumtux Chinook?"— do you understand Chinook?

"Nika kumtux yaka"— I know him.

"Nika kumtux okoke"— I understand it, or I know that.

"Delate kumtux"— to know perfectly well, thorough knowledge, to prove, to be sure.

"Halo delate kumtux"— to be in doubt, uncertain.

"Halo kumtux" and "wake kumtux"— do not understand, to misunderstand, not to know.

"Iskum kumtux"— to get knowledge, to learn.

"Nika ticky kumtux"— I want to know; I desire to learn.

"Kumtux mamook"— to understand how it is done; to be skillfull or competent.

"Halo kumtux mamook"— unskilled; incompetent, don't know how to do it (mamook meaning work, the act of doing anything).

KUN'-A-MOKST (C): Both, together, with, amid, among, beside, besides, "all two."

"Kunamokst kahkwa"— both alike.

"Nesika klatawa kunamokst"— we will go together.

"Nika mitlite kunamokst yaka"— I live with him.

"Chako kunamokst"— to come together, to join or unite; to come with each other, meet, congregate, gather together, assemble.
"Wawa kunamokst"— talk together, consult.
"Tumtum kunamokst"— to agree in opinion.
"Kunamokst mika"— to agree with you.
KUN'-SIH or konsee (C): How many? how much? when, ever.
"Kunsih tillikum mitlite?"— how many people are there?
"Kunsih mika klatawa?"— when do you go?
"Wake kunsih"— not ever, never.
"Mamook kunsih"— to count, the act of ascertaining how many.
"Kunsih hyas?"— how big?
"Kunsih laly?"— how long?
"Kunsih dolla?"— how many dollars? what price or cost?
"Kunsih siah?"— how far? distance.
"Kunsih hiyu?"— how much.
"Kunsih mika chako?"— when did you come?
"Kunsih chaco Chautsh?"— when will George come?
"Wake kunsih"— never.
KUSH'-IS (S): Stockings, socks.
KWAD'-DIS (K): Whale (see Ekkoli).
KWAIST or kweest (C): Nine.
"Tahtlum pe kwaist"— ten and nine, is nineteen.
"Kwaist tahtlum"— nine tens, is ninety.
"Kwaist tukamonuk"— nine hundred.
KWA-LAL' KWA-LAL' (C): To gallop.
KWAL'-H (S): An aunt.
KWAN (C): Glad, merry, tame, meek, quiet.
"Yaka kwan"— he is glad.
KWASS (C): fear; to be afraid, tame, shy, timid; to fear, to tame.
"Halo kwass"— fearless, not afraid.
"Nika kwass"— I am afraid.
KWA'-TA (E): A quarter of a dollar. (Indian attempt to pronounce the word quarter.) "Tenas sitkum," small half, is another expression for the quarter or less than half of anything.
KWATES (S): Sour; bitter; not pleased.
KWEH-KWEH (J): A mallard duck.
KWEK'-WE-ENS (S): A pin.
KWELTH (S): Proud.
KWE'-O KWE'-O (C): A ring; a circle.
KWIN'-NUM (C): Five (the numeral).
"Tahtlum pe kwinnum"— ten and five, fifteen.
"Kwinnum tahtlum"— fifty.
KWI'-SE-O (C): The porpoise.
KWISH (C): Refusal (exclamation of).
KWIS'-KWIS (C): A squirrel (the red or pine squirrel).

KWIT'-SHAD-IE (S): Hare; rabbit.

KWO'-LAN (S): The ear.

"Kumtux kopa kwolan"— to hear.

"Halo kwolan"— deaf.

KWON'-E-SUM (C): Always, forever, eternal, continual, everlasting, perpetual, unceasing, etc.

"Kahkwa kwonesum"— like always, as usual.

"Kwonesum nika nanitch okoke"— always I see that.

"Kwonesum yaka klatawa"— always he goes.

"Kwonesum mitlite"— to keep, to remain permanently.

KWULT (C): To hit, strike, or wound (without cutting).

KWUN-NUM' (S): To count; numbers (see Kunsih).

KWUTL (C): To push; to squeeze; secure; fasten.

"Mamook kwutl chik-chik"— push the wagon hard.

L

LA-BLEED' (F): A bridle.

LA-BOOS' (F): Mouth (see la-push).

LA-BOO-TAI' (F): A bottle.

LA-CA'-LAT (F): A carrot.

LA-CA-SET' (F): A box, a trunk or chest, a casket, money-box.

LA-CLO'-A: (F): A cross.

LAGH (C): To tip, to lean, to stoop, to bend over; to tip, as a boat.

"Wake nika lagh canim"— I did not tip the canoe.

"Yahka lagh kahkwa oleman"— he stoops like an aged man.

LA-GOME' (F): Pitch, glue, gum.

"La-gome stick"— pitch-pine.

LA-HAL' (C): A game played with ten small disks, one of which is marked. The game was played by all Indians in the Northwest from immemorial times; it was the universal native pastime. It is primitive enough, consisting in successfully guessing the hand that holds the marked disk. "Mamook lahal" is to gamble and lahal is the name of the game. Among Puget Sound Indians and those farther north the word is commonly lahal, but in earlier times it was slahal for the bones and lahal for the disks, both devices being used among the tribes.

LA-HASH' (F): An ax or hatchet.

LAK'-IT (C): Four (the numeral).

LA-LAH' (C): To cheat, trick; joke with.

LA-LAHM' (F): An oar.

"Mamook lalahm"— to row, to use the oar.

LA-LANG' (F): The tongue, a language.

"Nika lalang huloima kopa yaka lalang"— my language is different from his language.

LA-LEEM' (F): A file.

LA-LIM' (F): Rasp, file.

LA'-LY (C): Time. (Prolonging the "a" sound in pronouncing "laly" means a long time, but do not confuse this with "ahnkuttie," which means former time, formerly, ago. The same distinction between time and long time in the pronunciation of "laly" is found in using the word "siah" for far. Prolonging the sound of "i" in "siah" means very far.)

"Tenas laly"— a short time.

"Kunsih laly"— how long?

"Tenas laly kimta"— a little while after.

"Tenas laly elip"— a little while before.

"Kunsih laly mika mitlite yukwa?"— How long have you lived here?

LA-MAH' (F): The hand, arm, thumb, fingers, sleeve, handle of anything, limb or knot of a tree.

"Kloshe lamah"— the right (good) hand.

"Potlatch lamah"— shake (give) hands.

"Iskum kopa yaka lamah"— get in his arm, to hug.

"Kimtah lamah"— elbow.

LA-MAI' (F): An old woman.

LA-MESSE' (F): The ceremony of the mass.

"Mamook la-messe"— to say mass. (The reason why it is not "wawa la-messe" — wawa, talk — is probably that the ceremony is an act, the priest at work, and mamook is the proper word for work, or for any act.)

LA-MET'-SIN (F): Medicine — but not in the sense of magic. ("Tahmah-nawis" is the term for magic, the medicine of the Indian conjurer, or medi-icine man. "La-metsin" is Jargon and is an Indian attempt to pronounce the French for medicine. It means drugs, salves, ointments, pills, powders, physics.)

"La-metsin tupso"— an herb.

"Mika ticky la-metsin?"— do you want medicine?

LA-MON'-TAY (F): A mountain.

"Klatawa kopa saghalie la-montay"— to ascend to the summit of the mountain.

LA-PEEP' (F): A tobacco pipe.

LA-PEHSH' (F): A pole.

LA-PELL' (F): A shovel or spade.

LA-PEL'-LAH (J): A roast.

"Mamook lapellah"— to roast before a fire, the act of roasting.

LA-PE-OSH' (F): A mattock or hoe.

LA-PLASH' (F): A plank, a board, lumber.

"Cultus laplash"— refuse or waste lumber.

"Laplash man"— a carpenter, a builder of houses, a worker in wood.

"Kah mika iskum okoke laplash?"— where did you get that lumber?

LA-PO-EL' (F): A frying pan; a stove.

"Mamook lapoel"— to fry.

LA-POME' (F): An apple.

"Chuck lapome"— cider.

LA-POOL′ (F): A hen; poultry.

"Siwash lapool"— the grouse.

LA-POTE′ (F): A door.

LA-PUSH′ or la-boos′ (F): The mouth, mouth of a river.

"Mokst laboos or lapush"— the forks of a river, literally, two mouths.

"Kloshe kopa lapush"— good to the mouth, hence to relish.

LA-PUSH′-ET (F): Hayfork.

LA-SAN-SHEL′ (F): Girth, sash, belt, strap.

LA-SEE′ (F): A saw.

LA-SELL′ (F): A saddle.

LA-SHAL-LOO′ (F): Plough.

LA-SHAN′-DEL (F): A candle.

LA-SHASE′ (F): Chair.

LA-SHEM′-I-NAY (F): The chimney.

LA-SHEN′ (F): A chain.

LA-SHEY′ (J): Barley.

LA-SI-ET′ (F): A plate.

LA-SWAY′ (F): Silk, silken.

LA-TAH′ (F): The teeth.

LA-TAHB′ (F): Table.

LA-TATE′ (F): The head, brains, sense, intellect.

"Pil latate"— red head.

"Nika sick kopa nika latate"— I am sick in my head.

"Halo latate"— no head, stupid.

"Kopa latate"— with the head, mental.

"Huloima latate"— different head, delirious.

"Tupso kopa latate"— hair; literally, the grass on the head.

"Wake skookum latate"— imbecile.

LA-TLAH′ (F): Noise.

"Skookum latlah"— loud.

LAW (E): Law, command, decree. (The Indians had tribal law exercised by themselves or through the commands and degrees of chieftains. Also there was Boston or American law. They found the short English word, law, easy, and it was adaptable into the Jargon.)

"Yaka kumtux Boston law"— he understands American law.

"Delate kopa law" or "kloshe kopa law"— legal.

"Wake kloshe kopa law"— illegal or illegitimate.

LA-WEN′ (F): Oats. (This grain was one of the earliest and most prolific crops produced in the Northwest when Indians were still numerous.)

LA-WEST′ (F): A vest or waistcoat.

LAW′-SUK (C): To dance, dance.

LA′-ZY (E): Lazy (see klawah).

LE-BAH′-DO (F): A shingle; shingles.

LE-BAL′ (F): Ball; a bullet.

"Tenas lebal"— little bullets or shot.

LE-BISK'-WEE (F): Biscuit.

LE-COO' (F): The neck.

LE-DOO' (F): Finger.

LE-KLEH' (F): A key.

"Mamook lekleh"— make locked, lock the door.

"Mahsh lekleh"— unlocked.

"Mamook halo lekleh"— unlocked, also; literally, make not locked.

LE-KYE' (F): Spotted, mottled, dappled.

LE-LO'-BA (F): Ribbon.

LE-LOO' (F): The big gray wolf.

LE-MAH'-TO (F): A hammer.

LE-MEL' or le-mool' (F): A mule.

LE-MO'-LO (F): Wild, untamed, skittish, barbarous. (Not much used after the natives learned the world wild.)

LE-MOO'-TO (F): Sheep.

"Klootchman lemooto"— ewe.

"Lemooto house"— fold, sheepfold.

LE-MOSH' (F): Flies.

LE-PAN" (F): Bread; a loaf of bread.

LE-PEE' (F): The feet, a foot, leg, thigh, a paw, foot prints, tracks; formerly pronounced luh-pe-ay.

"Yaka lepee yaka kokshut"— his leg is broken.

"Kah lepee mitlite"— footstep; where foot is or was.

"Klatawa kopa lepee"— go on foot, walk.

"Tzum kah lepee mitlite"— mark where foot was; track.

LE-PI-EGE' (F): A trap or snare.

LE-PISH'-E-MO (J): The saddle blanket and trappings of a horse.

LE-PLAH' (F): Plate or dishes.

LE-PLET' (F): A priest, preacher, minister.

"Yahwa klatawa nesika leplet"— there goes our minister.

One authority, Louis St. Onge (1873) cites a number of church terms used in the Jargon including:

"Lesepek"— bishop.   "Lesapot"— apostle.
"Paska"— Easter.   "Olo time"— Lent.
"Eklis"— church.   "Katolik"— Catholic.
"Sesu Kli"— Jesus Christ.

However, the only Indian pronunciation the present writer ever heard for Jesus was "Chesus." The "Sesu Kli" of St. Onge sounds more like a Chinese attempt to say those words. The early Chinese placer miners and camp cooks all used the Jargon as easily as the whites or Indians, and used it in preference to attempting to talk English.

LE-PWAH' (F): Peas.

LE-SAI' (F): Saint.

LE-SAK' (F): A bag, a pocket, a sack.

LE-SEE'-ZO (F): Scissors; shears.

LE-WHET' (F): A whip.
  "Mamook le-whet"— to whip.
LE-YAUB' (F): The devil (see deaub).
LICE (E): (Indian attempt to say rice.)
LIP'-LIP (J): To boil.
  "Mamook liplip"— to make boil or cause to boil.
  "Okoke lice yaka liplip alta"— that rice it boils now.
LOK'-IT or lakit (C): Four (the numeral).
LO'-LO (C): To carry, bring, bear, load, fetch, remove, transfer, pack, convey, lug, renew. (Originally, lolo meant to carry a child on the back).
  "Mamook lolo kopa canim"— make load into canoe.
  "Kloshe mika lolo okoke iktas"— load those things good or well, properly.
LOPE (E): Rope.
  "Tenas lope"— a cord.
  "Skin lope"— rawhide.
LO-WUL-LO (C): Round, whole, all of anything.
LUK'-UT-CHEE (F): Clams. (This word is applied only to the hardshell or little-neck clam. The quahang or large, round clam of Puget Sound is called "smetock" on the northern coasts, and the largest of all "go-duck.")
LUM (E): Rum, whiskey, spirits. (The Indian rendition of "r".)
  "Lumpechuck"— grog (rum and water).

M

MAH'-KOOK (N): To buy or sell, a purchase, a bargain. Originally, to trade or exchange. (see "huyhuy" for a discussion of the use of this word.)
  "Hyas mahkook"— dear.
  "Tenas mahkook"— cheap.
  "Kah mika mahkook okoke iktas?"— where did you buy those things?
  "Nika ticky mahkook iktas"— I want to buy some things.
  "Mahkook house"— a store, trading post.
MAH'-LIE (N): To forget.
MAHSH (F): Leave, turn out, throw away, acquit, banish, cast, dash, desert, dispatch, dismiss, distribute, detach, drop, apply, expel, to part with, remove, exterminate, extinguish, fling, forsake, get rid of, heave, hurl, lay down, omit, insert, pour, put, reject, release, relinquish, remit, send, sling, sow, spill, spend, thrust, toss, transmit — and probably others. (Also to sell, see huyhuy.)
  "Mahsh chuck kopa boat"— bail out the boat; remove the water from the boat.
  "Nika mahsh nika kuitan"— I have sold my horse.
  "Cultus mahsh"— to waste.
  "Halo mahsh"— to hold, not waste or throw away or leave.
  "Tenas mahsh"— to move.
  "Mahsh!"— get out.

"Mahsh keekwullie"— to lower, or put below, to inject, sink, enclose, throw down, put inside.

"Mahsh tenas"— to give birth to a child.

"Mahsh kunamokst"— mix, put all together.

"Mahsh kopa illahee"— bury, put into the ground.

"Mahsh puss-puss klahanie house"— put the cat out.

"Mahsh okoke pish"— throw that fish away.

MAH'-SIE (F): Thank you, thanks, thankful; also to pray.

"Kloshe nesika mahsie kopa Saghalie Tyee"— let us pray to God; literally, "good we pray to God".

"Wawa mahsie"— to give thanks, to praise.

"Mahsie kopa Saghalie Tyee"— praise to God — the Doxology.

MAHT'-LIN-NIE (C): Off shore; out at sea. (Used two ways: if in a boat it is then to keep off; if on land it is to go toward the water.)

MAH'-TWIL-LIE (C): In shore, shoreward, on land, towards the interior. (The opposite of mahtlinnie.)

MA'-KE-SON (J): The chin.

MA-LAH' (C): Tinware, earthenware, dishes.

MAL'-LIE (E): To marry, get married; matrimony, marriage, wedding. (An Indian attempt to say marry.)

"Yaka mallie alta"— he is married now.

"Alta nika klatawa kopa mallie"— now I am going to the wedding.

"Elip kopa mallie"— before the wedding, ante nuptial.

"Man yaka chee mallie"— bridegroom, or man newly married.

"Klootchman yaka chee mallie"— a bride.

"Kokshut mallie"— a divorce, literally a broken marriage.

MAL-TEE'-NY (J): Near at hand.

MA-MA (E): Mamma.

MAM-OOK (N): To make, to do, to work, the act of doing anything, action, labor, exertion, act, deed, work, job, task, toil.

This is the one word in the Jargon that denotes action or which distinguishes the act. It is the most useful word in the Jargon as it is prefixed to many nouns, verbs and adjectives and makes them active verbs. Among the Indians on Puget Sound it was the most common Chinook (Jargon) word in use.

"Mamook chako"— make to come or bring, to fetch.

"Mamook liplip"— make to boil.

"Ikta mika mamook?"— what are you doing?

"Mamook elip"— to begin.

"Mamook kloshe"— to make good.

"Mamook tumtum"— to think, to reason.

"Mamook tzum"— to write.

"Mamook alki"— to delay, to make by and by.

"Mamook cultus"— to make bad or no good.

"Mamook kahkwa"— to imitate or mimic, make like.

"Mamook delate"— to make right or correct.

"Mamook killapi"— to twist or make twisted or crooked, to turn over, to withdraw.

"Mamook kopet"— to stop check, finish, conclude, extinguish.

"Mamook kow"— to tie or wrap, hitch, confine, strap, capture or fasten.

"Mamook kumtux"— to teach, explain, illustrate, inform, make understand.

"Mamook kunsih"— to count; literally, to make how many.

"Mamook sick tumtum"— to ill treat and hurt one's feelings.

"Mamook skookum"— to strengthen, to make strong, to invigorate.

"Mamook skookum tumtum"— to make brave or courageous.

"Mamook haul"— must.

"Chee mamook"— new work, beginning something.

"Cultus mamook"— poor work, bad work.

"Delate kumtux mamook"— knowing how to work.

"Halo delate mamook"— not right work.

"Kumtux mamook"— skill, knowing the work.

"Kwonesum mamook"— always working, striving, persevering.

"Potlatch mamook"— to give work, employment, to hire.

"Ticky mamook"— desire or want work.

MAN (E): Man. (Also the male of any animal.)

"Tenas man"— lad.

"Man eena" —a male beaver.

"Tenas man moolack"— a little buck elk. (however, stallion is "stone kuitan")

MEL'-A-KWA (F): A mosquito.

ME-LASS' (E): Molasses (Less common than silup or syrup. Both are Indian attempts to pronounce the English words).

MEM'-A-LOOSE (C): Dead, to die, expire, decay, become rotten, extinguish.

"Chako memaloose"— become rotten, decay.

"Mamook memaloose"— to kill, murder, execute.

"Memaloose kopa chuck"— to drown, die in the water.

"Memaloose illahee"— a grave or a graveyard, a tomb.

ME-SA'-CHIE (C): Bad, wicked, evil, vile; sin, vice, iniquity. (Not in the sense of cultus, which is worthless.)

"Elip mesachie"— worse.

"Elip mesachie kopa konaway"— worse than all, worst.

"Mesachie mitlite"— danger, the place where bad is.

ME-SI'-KA (C): You, your, yours. (Second person, plural number, all cases.)

MI'-KA (C): You, your, yours, thee, thine. (Anything pertaining to the second person singular, all cases.)

"Okoke mika kuitan?"— is this your horse?

"Kah mika klatawa?"— where are you going?

MI'-MIE (C): Downstream.

MIST-CHI'-MAS (J): Slave.

MIT-ASS' (CR): Leggings.

MIT'-LITE (C): To stay at, to reside, remain, sit, sit down, to have, inhabit, abide, dwell, exist, be present, recline, keep, possess, wait. (It is also used for the impersonal verb to be, is.)
"Kah mika mitlite?"— where do you live?
"Mitlite kopa house"— is in the house.
"Yaka mitlite kopa yaka house"— he is in his house.
"Cultus mitlite"— to stop or stay anywhere without any particular purpose.
"Halo mitlite"— to be absent.
"Kunsih mitlite?"— how many remain?
"Mitlite tenas"— to be with child.
"Mitlite kopa chuck"— to be wet.

MIT'-WHIT (C): To stand, stand up, arise, be erect.
"Mitwhit stick"— a standing tree, a mast.
"Kloshe mesika mitwhit"— please arise; literally, good you stand up, the plural mesika showing that it is addressed to an audience or assemblage.

MOKST or moxt (C): Two, twice, double, pair, couple, second.
"Mokst klootchman"— two women.
"Mokst tahtlum"— twenty, twice ten.
"Mokst tumtum"— of two minds, consequently in doubt.

MOO'-LA (F): A mill or factory.
"Laplash moola"— a saw mill.
"Sapolil moola"— a flour mill.

MOO'-LACK (C): An elk.

MOON (E): The moon, a month.
"Ikt moon"— one month.
"Chee moon"— new moon.
"Sick moon"— the waning or old moon.
"Kopa mokst moon nika killapi"— in two months I will return.

MOOS'-MOOS (J): Cattle, beef, buffalo.
The word is of doubtful origin. It occurs in almost that form in the Cree, which is moostoos, and is their word for buffalo. There were neither buffalo nor cattle in the Pacific Northwest country, but buffalo and buffalo skins were brought over from the Yakima country in old Indian days. Undoubtedly the word came with them, and when cattle were introduced, the tribes imitated the Cree as closely as possible. Hence we have moostoos (Cree), musmus (Yakima), musmus (Klickitat), musmus (Chinook) and moosmoos (Jargon).
"Yaka mitlite taghum moosmoos"— he has six cattle.
"Man yaka kumtux mamook memaloose moosmoos"— a butcher; a man who knows how to kill cattle.

MOO'-SUM (S): Sleep, slumber, asleep; to sleep.
"Nika ticky moosum"— I am sleepy; I want to sleep.
"Nika hyas moosum"— I slept soundly.
"Yaka moosum alta"— he sleeps now.

"Mamook tenas moosum"— to go to bed together, but not to sleep; make little sleep.

MOW'-ITCH (N): A deer, venison. (The word is frequently used to mean any animal.)

"Klootchman mowitch"— a doe.

"Huloima mowitch"— an animal that is strange or different.

MUCK'-A-MUCK (J): Food, nutriment, meal, feast, eat; to eat, bite, chew, browse, devour. (Muckamuck is to take anything into the mouth.)

"Muckamuck sapolil"— to eat bread.

"Muckamuck chuck"— to drink water.

"Mamook piah muckamuck"— to cook food.

"Potlatch muckamuck"— to give food or feed.

"Muckamuck kopa polaklie"— supper, food at night.

"Muckamuck kopa sitkum sun"— the midday meal, food at half of the day.

"Muckamuck kopa tenas sun"— the meal when the sun is young, the early morning meal, breakfast.

"Halo muckamuck"— famine.

MUS'-KET (E): A gun or musket.

MY-EE'-NA (C): To sing; a song.

N

NA? (J): An interrogative interjection.

"Sick na mika?"— are you sick?

NAH! (S): Look, ha, look here, hey, look there, hark, listen. An interjection. An original Indian word common to several of the native languages.

"Nah sikhs!"— hey friend!

"Nah tillikums!"— hark people!

NA-HA' (C): Mother. (rarely used, the English mamma having superseded it.)

NAN'-ITCH (N): See, to see, look, to look for, seek, observe, glance, view, behold.

"Kloshe nanitch"— look out, be careful, look well; literally, good look.

"Cultus nanitch"— to look around idly, from curiosity.

"Mamook nanitch"— to show, to make seen.

NAU'-ITS (S): Off shore; on the stream, the sea-beach.

NA-WAM'-OOKS (C): Sea otter.

NEM (E): Name.

"Mamook nem"— to name, to call by name.

"Kloshe nem"— a good name, to honor.

"Hyas kloshe nem"— a very great name.

NE-NAM'-OOKS (C): The land otter.

NES'-I-KA (C): We, our, ours, us. (First person, plural, all cases.)

"Chako kopa nesika"— come to (or with) us.

"Alta nesika klatawa"— now we will go.

"Nesika kuitan delate till"— our horses are very tired.

NEW'-HAH (C): Here, hither, to this place (see yukwa).

NI'-KA (C): I, me, my, mine. (First person singular, all cases.) The personal pronouns become possessive by prefixing them to nouns:
"Nika nem"— my name.
"Mika kuitan"— your horse.
"Nesika illahee"— our land.
"Nika house"— my home.

Sometimes "s" is added to the personal pronouns in the possessive case:
"Nikas"— mine.   "Mikas"— yours.
"Nesikas"— ours.   "Mesikas"— yours.
"Yakas"— his or hers.   "Klaskas"— theirs.

This mode is used generally only when the pronoun is the last word in the sentence, thus: "Okoke kuitan nikas"— that horse is ours.
"Nika nanitch yaka"— I see him.
"Yaka kokshut nika"— he hit me.
"Nika klootchman"— my wife or woman.
"Nika tenas man"— my son, little man, boy, or if used by a young woman, may mean my sweetheart.
"Nika tenas klootchman"— my little woman, daughter, girl, sweetheart.
"Nika tumtum"— I think; my thought, guess or opinion.
"Nika tumtum kahkwa"— I agree, I think so, I think like that, I approve.

NOSE (E): Nose. Also used for a promontory, point of land, a spit, the bow of a boat or canoe.

NOW'-IT-KA or naw-it-ka (C): Yes, aye, assuredly, indeed.
"Nowitka, nika klatawa"— yes, I will go.
"Nowitka, wake nika kumtux"— indeed, I do not know.
"Klonas nowitka"— probably so, perhaps so; yes, maybe.
"Wawa nowitka"— say yes, acquiesce, assent.

O

OK'-CHOCK (J): Shoulders.

O'-KOKE (C): This, that, these, those.
"Ikta okoke?"— what is that?
"Okoke klaksta"— he, who or that or these who.
"Okoke klaska"— they.
"Okoke mitlite"— that remaining, the remainder, that which is left.
"Okoke polaklie"— tonight, this night.
"Okoke sun"— today, this day.

O-KUS'-TEE (C): A daughter.
"Nanitch, nika okustee"— look, my daughter.

O-LAL'-LIE (BB): Berries, fruit; originally, the salmon berry.
"Klale olallie"— blackberry.
"Pil olallie"— any red berry.
"Olallie chuck"— berry juice.
"Shot olallie"— huckleberries.
"Seahpo olallie"— raspberries.

O'-LA-PITS-KI (C): Fire.

OLE'-MAN (E): An old man; old, worn out, anything that is old.
"Okoke kuitan yaka hyas oleman"— that horse he is very old.
"Okoke canim yaka hyas oleman"— that canoe it is worn out.

OL'-HI-YU (C): A seal.

O'-LO (C): Hungry, hungry for.
"Olo chuck"— hungry for water, thirsty.
"Olo moosum"— sleepy, though "ticky moosum" is more often used,
meaning want sleep.
"Nika hyas olo alta"— I am very hungry now.

O'-LUK (S): A snake.

O'-NA (C): Clam; clams. (This word especially applied to "razor" clams.)

OO'-A-HUT or wayhut (C): A road, way, trail, path.
"Kah ooahut kopa Nisqually?"— where is the road to Nisqually?
"Ooahut kopa chuck"— a channel.
"Ooahut kopa town"— a street.
"Chuck ooahut"— to ford.

OO'-LA-CHAN (CL): A type of smelt. Sometimes called candlefish.

OOL'-CHUS (J): Herring; herrings.

OOS'-KAN: (C): A cup; a bowl.

O'-PE-KWAN (C): Basket; can, tin kettle.

O'-PITL-KEGH (C): Bow, (kalitan — arrow.)

O-PIT'-SAH (C): A knife; dagger.
(The table fork is sometimes called "opitsah sikhs," the "friend of the
knife." Opitsah sikhs is sometimes used to denote a lover—a fork to every
knife).

O-POOTS' or opootsh (C): The rear end, the tail of an animal, the rudder
of a boat, the posterior, the back, the backside, anus.
"Boat opoots"— the boat's rudder.
"Opoots sill"— a breech clout.
"Humm opoots"— a skunk, a stinking tail.

O-QUAN'-AX (C): The neck.

OTE'-LAGH (C): The sun.

OU-WUCH'-EH (C): A swan.

OW (C): A brother (younger than the speaker).
"Kah mika ow?"— where is your (younger) brother?
"Elip ow"— an elder brother.
"Kahkwa ow"— like a brother, fraternal.
"Ow yaka klootchman"— brother his wife, a sister-in-law.
"Ow yaka tenas man"— brother his son, a nephew.
"Ow yaka tenas klootchman"— brother his daughter, a niece.

Such expressions fairly illustrate the order of words and the combinations
of words used to express definite things and relationships. They are essentially Indian and not at all English. They originate with the Indian and
are the arrangements of words that are characteristic of most of the native
tongues.

P

PAHT'L (C): Full.

"Pahtlum"— drink; full of rum.

"Pahtl chuck"— wet; full of water.

"Pahtl illahee"— dirty.

"Mamook pahtl"— to fill or make full.

"Kwonesum yaka pahtlum"— he is always drunk; literally, always he full of rum. (Note the arrangement of words.)

PAINT or pent (E): Paint.

PAN (F): Bread.

"Mamook le pan"— knead.

PAPA (E): Papa or father.

"Nika nanitch yaka papa"— I see his father.

PA-SE'-SE (C): A blanket, woolen cloth.

"Tzum pasese"— a quilt. (Tzum means colors, stripes, pictures, writing.)

"Yaka mitlite kwinnum pasese"— he has five blankets.

PA-SI'-OOKS (C): A Frenchman.

This Jargon word is derived from "pasese" and "uks." The latter, "uks," is a plural applied to living beings, people. The Indians called the early whites clothmen. The French, who were with the Hudson's Bay Company, came to have the term applied to them only. Americans first came in ships from Boston, and the early English came during the reign of George III. They were known as Boston men and King Chautsh (George) men respectively, while the original Chinook word for men who wore cloth clothes, "pasiooks," was given to the French and became Jargon. All white men other than Americans, English and French were called Dutchmen by the natives, and it is still "Dutchman" in the Jargon.

P'-CHIH or pitchih (J): Thin, as of a board.

PE (F): And or but (occasionally means then, besides).

"Yaka pe nika klatawa"— he and I will go.

"Pe weght"— and also, and again.

"Pe kahta"— and why.

PE-CHUGH' (C): Green.

PEL'-TON (J): A fool, foolish, crazy, insane, an insane person.

It is supposed that the Indians adopted this term from the name of a deranged person, one Archibald Pelton or Felton. Wilson Price Hunt was said to have found this man in his travels and to have taken him to Astoria. This was before Hudson's Bay days, when whites were still new to the natives.

PEP'-AH (E): Paper, a letter, a book — anything written or printed.

"Mamook pepah"— to write.

"Kumtux pepah"— to read.

"Kloshe mika mamook pepah kopa nika"— please you write a letter for me.

"Saghalie tyee yaka pepah"— literally, God, his paper or book, the Bible.

PE-SHAK' (N): Bad; also occasionally danger. (Both "mesachie" and "cultus" are used for bad, "mesachie" in the sense of wicked or evil and "cultus" in the sense of no good or worthless.)

PE-WHAT'-TIE (C): Thin (like paper).

PI'-AH (E): Fire, blaze, flame, cooked, burned, ripe, mellow, or mature.
"Mamook piah"— make or build fire, cook, burn.
"Piah olallie"— ripe berries.
"Piah chuck"— fire water, whisky.
"Piah sapolil"— baked bread.
"Saghalie piah"— lightning, or literally fire above.
"Piah sick"— venereal disease, gonorrhea.

PIL (C): Red, or of a reddish color.
"Pil chikamin"— gold money; also the metals gold, brass, copper.
"Pil illahee"— red earth, ochre.
"Pil kuitan"— a bay horse.
"Pil okchok"— (red shoulders) — the blackbird.

PIL'-PIL (J): Blood.
"Hiyu pilpil chako"— much blood came.
"Mahsh pilpil"— to bleed, also to menstruate.

PISH (E): Fish. (The Indian could not pronounce f. His nearest approach was p. Hence pish for fish, and piah for fire.)
"Tenas pish"— minnow.
"Pishhook"— fishhook.

PIT-LILL' (J): Thick (like molasses).

PIU-PIU or pu-pu (E): Stench, stink. (Probable imitation of sound of disgust made over a bad smell. Piu-piu is an interjection. Humm is used in sentences.)

POH (C): A puff of breath; to blow.
"Mamook poh"— to blow out or extinguish, as a candle, or to fire a salute.

PO'-LAK-LIE (C): Night, dark, darkness, gloom like night.
"Tenas polaklie"— evening.
"Hyas polaklie"— very late at night.
"Sitkum polaklie"— midnight, half a night.
"Alta polaklie chako"— now night has come.
"Kimta sitkum polaklie"— after midnight.

PO'-LAL-LIE (J): Powder, gunpowder, dust, sand.
"Polallie illahee"— sandy ground.

POO (J): Imitation of the sound of a gun.
"Mamook poo"— to shoot.
"Mokst poo"— a double barrelled gun.

POO'-LIE (F): Rotten.
"Poolie lapome" —a rotten apple.

POT'-LATCH (N): A gift and to give. (When it denotes giving, it is a verb and when it is used for the gift itself or for the celebration, it is a noun.)
The potlatch was a native festival common to all the tribes of the North-

west. Its feature was the distribution of gifts. The most noted chief was he who held the largest potlatch and gave away the most valuable and largest number of presents.

"Potlatch muckamuck"— to give food.

"Potlatch kloshe wawa"— give good talk, to congratulate, to give good advice.

"Kloshe mika potlatch nika wawa kopa yaka"— a long roundabout way of saying to intercede; literally, good you give me talk for him.

"Potlatch kopa saghalie tyee"— give to God, dedicate, consecrate.

"Potlatch wawa"— give talk or make a speech.

"Cultus potlatch"— a gift without prospect of recompense — a "bad gift" in an Indian's view.

"Potlatch dolla"— pay, to pay.

POT'-SUK (C): Between.

POW'-IL (J): To swell.

POW'-ITSH (C): The native thornapple or crabapple.

POWS (J): Halibut.

PUK'-PUK (J): A blow from the fist or a fist fight. (Another of the invented words which are pure Jargon.)

"Mamook pukpuk"— to box.

"Pukpuk solleks"— to fight when angry.

PUSS'-PUSS (E): A cat. (This is sometimes and in some localities pronounced pishpish.)

"Hyas pusspuss"— a cougar or big cat.

S

SAG'-HA-LIE (C): Up, above, heaven, sky, celestial, top, uppermost, over, upwards. (This word is usually pronounced as if it were spelled sockalie by the whites, and sag-ha-lie by the Indians, with the g sound deep in the throat and a guttural rather than an aspirate h.)

"Mamook saghalie"— to lift (raise).

"Saghalie Tyee Yaka book"— the bible; literally, God, His book.

"Saghalie Tyee Yaka wawa"— a sermon or religious talk; literally, God, His talk.

"Saghalie Tyee"— God, the Chief above, the ruler over all. (Saghalie Tyee, for the Deity or Jehovah, is a term invented by the early missionaries as none of the tribes had a word for God. They had their personal spirits but no universal Deity. Their first ideas of God came from the teachings of these missionaries. Christ is called in Jargon, "Saghalie Tyee Yaka tenas"— God, His Son.

SAIL (E): Sail; any cotton or linen cloth.

"Mamook sail"— to make sail.

"Mamook keekwullie sail"— to take in sail.

"Tzum sail"— printed cloth like calico (as is "tzum pasese," which really means quilt.)

"Snass sail"— oil cloth, rain cloth.

SAK'-O-LEKS (C): Trousers, pants.
"Keekwullie sakoleks"— drawers, underpants.
"Klahanie sakoleks"— overalls.
SAL'-AL (C): The salal shrub or its berries.
The salal is a beautiful evergreen shrub, growing abundantly along the Pacific Coast, with edible dark-purple berries about the size of the common grape. Before the coming of the white man, it was one of the most valued native fruits, and was gathered in large quantities by the coastal tribes. From it they made a sort of syrup, or dried and stored it in the form of thick cakes.
SALT (E): Salt or salty in taste.
"Salt chuck"— salt water, the sea.
"Salt chuck tupso"— sea weed.
SAM'-MON (E): Salmon (but usually written sammon in the Jargon).
"Tyee sammon"— (specifically) the King salmon of northern sounds and straits.
"Cultus sammon"— the kelts or spent salmon of the rivers in autumn and winter.
Tzum sammon"— steelhead and other trouts.
SAN'-DE-LIE (F): Ash-colored.
SAP'-O-LIL (C): Bread, wheat, grain, flour or meal.
"Piah sapolil"— baked bread.
"Hiyu sapolil"— much bread or flour.
SE'-AH-PO (F): A hat or cap.
"Klootchman seahpo"— a woman's hat or bonnet.
SE-AT'-CO (Ch): A goblin or nocturnal demon, greatly feared by the Coast Indians.
SEED (E): Seed.
SEE'-O-WIST (C): The eyes, the face, forehead.
"Halo seeowist"— blind.
"Ikt seeowist"— one-eyed.
"Lakit seeowist"— four eyes, spectacles.
"Dolla seeowist"— spectacles also, because the lenses are dollar shaped.
"Nika nanitch yaka kopa nika seeowist"— I saw him with my eyes.
"Chuck kopa seeowist"— tears, water of the eyes.
SE-LOKE'-MIL (J): A window.
SHAN'-TIE (F): To sing.
SHE'-LIP-O (C): Freeze, frozen.
SHE-LOK'-UM (C): Lookingglass, glass.
SHEM (E): Shame. (An Indian attempt to say shame).
"Halo shem"— without shame, shameless.
"Halo shem mika?"— no shame you? aren't you ashamed?
"Mamook shem"— to deride or ridicule and make ashamed.
SHU'-GAH (E): Sugar, honey, sweetening.
SHUGH (C): A rattle.
SHUGH-O'-POOTS (C): A rattlesnake, literally, the rear-end rattles.

SHUT (E): A shirt.
SHWAH'-KUK (S): A frog.
SI-AH' (N): Far, far off, away, afar, distant, remote.
John Jewitt recorded that the Nootkans also used siah for sky. To the
Nootkan the sky might have been just "the far off." For "very far off" the
word is sometimes repeated—siah-siah — but the usual method is to express
very great distance by prolonging the last syllable and saying si-a-h.
 "Nika klatawa siah"— I will go far off.
 "Siah"— far.
 "Delate siah"— a very great distance.
 "Elip siah"— farther.
 "Elip siah kopa konaway"— farther than all, farthest.
 "Wake siah"— not far.
 "Wake siah kopa"— almost or not far from.
SI-AM' (C): The grizzly bear. The grizzly is also called siam itswoot .
SICK (E): Sick.
 "Sick tumtum"— sad, grieved.
 "Mamook sick tumtum"— to hurt one's feelings.
 "Sick kopa kwolan"— earache.
 "Waum sick, cole sick"— fever and ague.
SIKHS or six (C): A friend or companion and used only toward men.
 "Klahowya sikhs"— how are you, friend?
 "Opitsah sikhs"— fork or friend of the knife.
Sikhs is also used as an equivalent for sweetheart, for which term there
is no single word in Jargon. "Nika tenas klootchman" is used for sweet-
heart as well as for daughter.
SIL'-UP (E): Syrup.
SIN'-A-MOKST or sinamoxt (C): Seven (the numeral).
SI'-PAH (W): Straight, like a ramrod.
SIS'-KI-YOU (Cr): A bob-tailed horse.
SIT'-KUM (C): Half, the middle.
 "Sitkum siwash"— half Indian, a half-breed.
 "Sitkum dolla"— half a dollar.
 "Elip sitkum"— more than half.
 "Tenas sitkum"— less than half.
 "Sitkum sun"— moon.
 "Elip sitkum sun"— forenoon.
SIT'-LAY (F): Stirrup.
SIT'-SHUM (S): To swim.
SI'-WASH (F): An Indian or aborigine, a savage. This is not a tribal name
as some uninformed writers have the impression when they erroneously
speak of "Siwash Indians."
 "Okoke siwash klootchman"— that is an Indian woman.
 "Hiyu siwash mitlite yukwa"— many Indians are here.
SKAD (J): A mole.

SKET-SOT'-WA (J): The Columbia river. This name was indicative of the "lower" river.

SKIN (E): Skin, hide, pelt, fur, leather.
"Skin shoes"— moccasins.
"Stick skin"— the bark of a tree.

SKOOKUM (S): Strong, powerful, potent. Originally, a ghost, evil spirit or demon.
This is one of the best known, most widely used and significant words in the Jargon. Its adoption by people of the Northwest has made of it a regional English word. There are many Skookum brands of Northwest-made goods. In fact, it is so common on the Pacific Coast as to have almost lost its Indian significance.
"Skookum town"— city.
"Skookum tumtum"— a brave spirit.
"Skookum chuck"— rapids.
"Skookum house"— a jail.

SKWAK'-WAL (S): A lamprey eel.

SKWISS-KWIS (J): The chipmunk or striped squirrel.

SLA-HAL' (C): An Indian game (see la-hal).

SMET'-OCKS (S): The large clam.

SMOKE (E): Smoke, clouds, fog, steam.

SNASS (J): Rain. A made word.
"Cole snass"— snow.
"Kull snass"— ice.

SOAP (E): Soap.

SO-LE'-MIE (C): The cranberry.

SOL'-LEKS (J): Anger, malice, hate, hatred, hostile, sulky, sullen, or any meaning that relates to anger.
"Mamook solleks"— to make mad, to provoke anger, resent, offend.
"Halo solleks"— not angry, meek, mild, pleasant.
"Yaka solleks kopa mika"— he is mad at you.
"Solleks wawa"— a quarrel with words, quarrelsome or fighting talk.
"Hiyu solleks" or "Hyas solleks"— very angry.
"Solleks wawa"— grumble.
"Solleks tillikum"— a mob.

SO'-PE-NA (C): To jump, hop, skip, spring.

SPO'-OH (C): Faded; any light color.

SPOON (E): A spoon.

SPOSE (E): Suppose, supposing, if, that, in order that, for. (See klonas to note the distinction between klonas and spose, which are sometimes confused by the novice.)
"Kloshe spose"— good if.
"Kahkwa spose"— as if.
"Spose nika klootchman memaloose"— if my wife dies.
"Nika kwass nika klootchman klonas memaloose"— I fear my wife perhaps will die.

STICK (E): A stick, a tree, pole, rod, wood.
"Stick skin"— bark.
"Ship stick"— a mast.
"Ikt stick"— a yard measure.
"Mitwhit stick"— a standing tree.
"Kull stick"— hardwood (oak).
"Isick stick"— paddle or oar wood (ash).
"Moos-moos stick"— goad.
STOCK'-EN (E): Stocking, sock.
STOH (C): Loose.
"Mamook stoh"— to make loose, to loosen or untie, absolve.
"Mamook stoh kahmooks"— let loose the dogs.
STONE (E): Stone or rock. Also signifies bone or horn.
"Stone kuitan"— a stallion.
STOTE'-KIN (C): Eight (the numeral).
STUTCH'-IN (E): Sturgeon. (An Indian attempt to pronounce the English word.)
SUK-WAL'-WAL (C): A gun.
SUN (E): Sun, a day, the sun.
"Okoke sun"— today.
"Ikt sun"— first day, Monday.
"Mokst sun"— Tuesday.
"Tenas sun"— early in the day.
"Sitkum sun"— noon, a half day.
"Tahlkie sun"— yesterday.
"Ikt tahlkie sun"— day before yesterday.
"Elip sitkum sun"— before noon.
"Kimta sitkum sun"— after noon.
"Sun yaka waum alta"— the sun is warm now.
"Sun chako"— daybreak.
SUNDAY (E): Sunday.
"Hyas Sunday"— a holiday.
"Ikt Sunday"— a week.

T

TAGH'-UM (C): Six (the numeral).
TAH (C): A spirit or supernatural thing or person.
TAHL'-KIE (C): Yesterday.
"Yaka chako tahlkie"— he came yesterday.
"Tahlkie moon"— last month.
"Tahlkie waum illahee"— last summer.
"Tahlkie cole illahee"— last winter.
TAH-MAH'-NA-WIS (C): A guardian or familiar spirit in its personal application. Every Indian had his tahmahnawis.
Tahmahnawis also means magic, ghost, spirit, or anything supernatural, and is used as the equivalent of luck, fortune and kindred words. It was

applied to anything the Indians could not readily understand.

"Mamook tahmahnawis"— conjure, make magic.

"Masachie tahmahnawis"— evil spirits, witchcraft.

"Klale tahmahnawis"— black magic, the devil, literally, dark or black spirit. The word is used as a noun, a verb or as an adjective according to whether it means a spirit is invoking the supernatural, or is ascribing magic powers either to men or to some object used as a charm.

TAH'-NESS (C): Knee.

TAH'-NIM (S): To measure.

TAHT'-LUM (C): Ten (the numeral).

TAL'-A-PUS (C): The coyote or prairie wolf. (The coyote is prominent in Indian mythology, which regards the creature as being of supernatural powers.)

"Hyas opoots talapus"— the fox; literally, big-tail coyote.

TAL'-IS (C): Dear, beloved.

TA-MO'-LITSH (C): A tub, bucket, barrel, cask, or keg.

"Ikt tamolitsh"— a bushel.

"Chuck mitlite kopa tamolitsh"— water is in the barrel or keg.

TA-NI'-NO (C): Crevasse, canyon, the vulva.

TANSE (E): Dance.

TA-TOOSH' (C): The breasts of a female, milk, udder, bosom, teats.

"Kloshe tatoosh"— cream.

"Tatoosh glease or lakles"— butter. (The words glease and lakles are from the English and French respectively. However, glease, for grease, fat or oil, is more commonly used than lakles.)

"Kull tatoosh"— cheese.

Tatoosh is the name of a range of mountains near Mount Rainier and it is also the name of an island off Cape Flattery.

TEA (E): Tea.

TE-AH'-WIT (C): The leg or foot.

"Klatawa teahwit"— to walk, go on foot.

"Klook teahwit"— lame, crooked leg (Klook was the Indian attempt to say the English word crooked).

TEH-TEH (C): To trot, as a horse.

TEL'-E-MIN (J): Ribs.

TEN'-AS (N): Small, few, little, a little, pretty, slight, a child, the young of an animal.

"Tenas snow chako"— little snow has come.

"Chako tenas"— to grow less, to decrease, diminish; literally, come small. "Mamook tenas" is another way of expressing the same idea.

"Hyas tenas"— very small.

"Tenas hiyu"— little much, some, several, a few.

"Tenas ahnkuttie"— recently, not very long ago, literally, small time ago.

"Chik-chik kopa tenas"— a baby carriage or wagon for a child.

"Tenas polaklie"— evening.

"Tenas yaka tenas"— a grandchild.

"Tenas house"— hut.

TEN'-TOME (Ch): Navel.

TE-PEH' (C): Quill, wing.

TICK'-Y (C): To want or desire, wish, be eager for, choose, pick, like, love. Also, it is used to express what one should want to do.

"Mika ticky muckamuck mika lametsin"— you should or must take your medicine.

"Ikta mika ticky?"— what do you want?

"Hyas ticky"— to long for or desire deeply.

"Delate halo ticky"— very much not like; therefore, to detest or dislike.

"Ticky kumtux"— want to know, to inquire.

TIK'-TIK (J): A watch (imitation of the sound).

TILL (J): Tired, heavy, fatigue, weight, weigh.

"Kunsih till okoke?"— how much does that weigh?

"Mamook till"— to weigh. Also to make tired or heavy with fatigue.

"Wake till"— not heavy, light.

"Nika hyas till"— I am very tired.

TIL'-LI-KUM (C): People, population, persons, tribe, nation, folks, friends, associates, relations, kin. (It usually means those who are not chiefs—the people, any people.)

"Nika tillikum"— my people.

"Yaka tillikum"— his people. (It is also used with a final s for the plural, although it was not originally so.)

"Yaka klatawa kopa yaka tillikums"— he has gone to his people.

"Nesika tillikums"— our people.

"Ahnkuttie tillikums"— former people, ancestors, forefathers.

"Huloima tillikums"— strangers, different people from our people.

"Hiyu tillikums"— a crowd, many people.

TIN'-TIN (J): A bell, the strike of an hour, a musical instrument, any musical instrument, music (imitation of the sound.)

"Mamook tintin"— to ring a bell, to make sounds on a musical instrument.

"Kunsih tintin alta?"— what time is it now?

"Ikt tintin"— one hour.

T-KOPE' (C): White or light colored.

"T'kope tillikums"— white people.

"Okoke pishpish yaka t'kope"— that cat is white.

(Also T'kopet. The latter is used as well as T'kope.)

TLAK'-TLAK (J): Grasshopper.

TLE-PAIT' (C): Nerve; nerves.

TL-KOPE' (C): To cut, hew or chop.

TOH (J): To spit. (A manufactured word.)

TOKE-TIE (Cal): Pretty.

"Hyas toketie kulla kulla"— a very pretty bird.

"Toketie tenas"— a good child.

TO'-LO (Cal): To earn, to gain, to win, prevail, control, convince, overcome, subdue, subject, defeat, triumph, manage, succeed, conquer.
"Kunsih dolla nika tolo spose nika mamook?"— how many dollars will I earn if I work?
"Wawa pe tolo"— to persuade.
"Nika tolo yaka"— I prevailed over him, I beat him, won over him.
TO'-LUKS (Clal): The mussel.
TO-MOL'-LA (E): Tomorrow.
"Ikt tomolla" or "Kopet tomolla"— day after tomorrow.
TOPE'-CHIN (J): A patch; to patch.
TOT (S): Uncle.
TO'-TO (C): To shake, sift, winnow.
TO-WAGH' or te-wagh (C): Bright, shining, light; daylight, light of a lamp or fire.
TO'-WAH (C): The nails, (fingernails and toenails).
TPISH'-KUKS (C): Flounder (fish).
T-SAK' (C): To stanch.
"Mamook tsak"— to stanch a wound.
TSA'-LIL (C): A lake.
T-SEE' (C): Sweet.
TSEE'-PE (Cal): To miss a mark, to mistake one's road, to make a mistake in speaking; to err, delude, blunder, or deceive, false, illusive, deceitful.
"Tseepe ooahut"— to take a wrong road.
"Tseepe mamook"— a trick, done deceitfully.
"Mamook tseepe"— to do deceitfully, to fool or delude.
"Tseepe wawa"— to mispronounce.
TSHI'-KE (C): Directly, soon.
T-SHISH' (C): Cold.
"Hiyu tshish okoke sun"— it is very cold today.
TSI-'A-LITS (C): A branch.
TSI-AT'-KO (S): A night-roving demon much feared by all the still superstitious Indians.
TSIK'-TSIK (J): A wagon or cart. (see chik-chik.)
T-SISH' (J): Imitation of the sound of a grindstone.
TSOLE'-PAT (K): A shotpouch.
TSO'-LO (Cal): To wander; to lose the way.
T-SUGH' (C): A crack or split.
"Mamook tsugh"— split.
"Chako tsugh"— to become split or cracked.
"Mamook tsugh illahee"— to plow the ground.
TUK-A-MO'-NUK (C): A hundred.
TUK'-WIL-LA (Cal): Nuts; the hazel nut.
TUM'-TUM (J): The heart, the will, opinion, belief, mind, memory, thought, purpose, intention, plan, etc.
(A widely used and variously employed word, one of the most expressive

in the Jargon, almost wholly used subjectively. Supposed to be a manufac-
tured word made to imitate the sound of the heart beat.)
  "Mahsh tumtum"— to give orders.
  "Mamook tumtum"— to make up one's mind, to think, plan or decide.
  "Sick tumtum"— grief.
  "Mokst tumtum nika"— undecided, two minds have I.
  "Halo tumtum"— without a will or an opinion.
  "Skookum tumtum"— bold, brave, strong heart, indomitable.
  "Ikta mika tumtum?"— what do you think?
  "Mika tumtum"— as you please.
  "Kahkwa nika tumtum"— as I think, or like I think.
  "He-he tumtum"— jolly.
TUM'-WA-TA (J&E): A waterfall (part imitation and part English. see
  tumtum).
TUP'-SHIN (S): A needle.
TUP'-SO (C): Grass, leaf or leaves, fringe, fur, feathers, hair, beard.
  "Kloshe tupso"— flowers.
  "Tupso illahee"— prairie or grassy country.
  "Tupso kopa latet"— hair.
T-WAH' (J): Shining, bright (towagh).
TY-EE' (N): A chief, only, in the old days, now a chief, a superior, a boss,
  an officer, a master, a gentleman, a foreman, a manager, anything superior.
  "Saghalie Tyee"— God.
  "Tyee sammon"— the largest variety of salmon in any given locality.
  "Kahkwa tyee"— kingly, like a king.
  "Tyee kopa Washington"— the president of the United States.
  "Klootchman tyee or tyee klootchman"— the matron of an Indian school.
TZUM (C): Mixed colors, spots, stripes, marks, figures, colors, printing, pic-
  tures, paint, painted, ornamental (gay colors).
  "Mamook tzum"— to write, draw, paint, dye, mark.
  "Tzum illahee"— surveyed land.
  "Tzum stick"— a pencil or brush for marking.
  "Tzum seeowist"— photograph.
  "Klale chuck kopa mamook tzum"— ink; literally, black water to make
  marks.
  "Tzum sammon"— trout.

U

U-AL'-TEE (C): Joy; gladness.
UL-A-LACH' (K): Wild onion; onion.
UL'-CHEY (C): The moose.
UL'-KEN or oo'-la-chan (Cl): A type of smelt.

W

WAGH (C): To spill, to vomit, to pour.
  "Mamook wagh chuck"— pour some water.

WAKE (N): No, not, none. (See halo—these terms are both used for the same meanings and purpose, and apparently without distinction, wake being without doubt the older form.)

"Nika wake kumtux"— I do not understand.

"Wake siah"— not far.

"Wake kloshe"— no good, not good.

"Wake hiyu"— not many, a few.

"Wake skookum"— not strong, weak, infirm, feeble.

"Wake kloshe kopa mahkook"— not good to sell, unsalable.

WAP'-PA-TO (J): The potato. (In earlier times the root of the *Sagittaria latifolia,* a native plant much esteemed by the natives and one of their regular sources of food supply. After the introduction of the potato the latter was called wappato and the former was known as siwash wappato, or Indian potato.)

WAUM (E): Warm (Indian attempt to say warm).

"Okoke sun yaka waum"— that sun it is warm, or today is warm, though for the latter the expression is usually inverted as: "Yaka waum okoke sun."

"Hyas waum" —hot.

"Waum sick, cole sick"— fever and ague.

WASH (E): Wash.

"Mamook wash"— to wash.

"Iskum wash"— to get washed, to be baptized.

WA'-WA (C): Speech, to talk, call, converse, conversation, sermon, story, tale, speak, declaim, voice, articulate. (It is anything that has to do with speech, whether written, printed or articulated.)

"Ikta mika wawa?"— what did you say?

"Delate wawa"— truth, fact, to promise.

"Hiyu wawa"— much talk, clamor, argument.

"Mahsh wawa"— to command or give orders.

"Killapi wawa"— to answer or reply.

"Kloshe wawa"— good talk, a proverb.

"Cultus wawa"— idle talk, jabber.

"Wawa kloshe"— to bless.

"Hyas wawa"— loud talk, boast, shout.

"Wawa halo"— to deny.

"Wawa kliminawhit"— to lie, untruthful statements.

"Wawa kopa Saghalie Tyee"— to pray or talk to God.

"Skookum wawa"— harangue.

WAY'-HUT (C): A road or trail (see ooahut).

WE-CO'-MA (C): The sea.

WEGHT or wekt (C): Again, also, more.

"Pe nika weght"— and I also.

"Weght nika klatawa"— again I go.

"Tenas weght"— a little more.

WHIM (N): Fallen; to fell.
"Whim stick"— a fallen tree.
"Mamook whim okoke stick"— fell this tree.
WIN'-A-PEE (N): By-and-by, presently. (Alki is more commonly in use.)
WIND (E): Wind; breath.
"Halo wind"— out of breath, dead.
"Skookum wind"— gale.
WIT'-KA (C): Now, at present time.
WOOT'-LAT (C): A phallus. (Often represented in carved pestles. Natural
pillars and towers of basalt were sometimes called "Wootlat," and vener-
ated. Rooster Rock was a notable wootlat.)

Y

YAH'-HUL (C): A name.
YAH'-WA (C): There, in that place, beyond, in that direction, yonder.
"Yaka mitlite yahwa"— he is there.
"Wake siah yahwa"— not far from there or thereabouts.
"Ikt yahwa, ikt yahwa"— one there, one there; apart, separated.
YA'-KA (C): He, his, him, she, her, hers, it, its (anything pertaining to the
third person, singular, all cases).
"Nika klook yaka teahwit"— my foot it is lame.
"Okoke kuitan yaka tkope"— the horse it is white.
"Yaka klatawa"— he has gone.
"Nanitch yaka"— see him.
YAK'-A-LA (C): Eagle.
YAK'-KIS-ILTH (C): Sharp, cutting.
YAK'-SO (C): Hair.
"Kuitan yakso"— mane.
YA-KWAH'-TIN (C): The belly, stomach, bosom.
"Keekwullie yakwahtin"— the entrails, within the belly.
"Yaka sick kopa yaka yakwahtin"— he is sick in the stomach; has the
stomachache.
YI'-EM (S): A tale or story, to relate a tale, to confess to a priest. (see wawa,
which was more commonly used.)
YOOTS (C): To sit.
YOTL (Ch): Glad, pleased, proud, spirited.
"Hyas yotl tumtum" or "Yaka tumtum delate kloshe"— his heart is very
glad.
YOTL'-KUT (C): Long (in dimension), length.
"Okoke stick hyas yotlkut"— this stick is very long.
YOT'-SKUT (C): Short.
"Yotskut capo"— jacket.
YUK'-WA (C): Here, this way, this side.
"Chako yukwa"— come here.
"Yukwa kopa okoke house"— this side of that house.

ENGLISH-CHINOOK

A

ABASE — mamook keekwullie.
ABDOMEN — yakwahtin; kwahtin.
ABED — kopa bed.
ABIDE — mitlite.
ABJECT — cultus.
ABLE — skookum.
ABOARD — kopa boat (or ship or canim).
ABOLISH — mamook halo.
ABORIGINE — siwash.
ABOUND — hiyu mitlite.
ABOUT — wake siah kopa.
ABOVE — saghalie.
ABSCOND — kapswolla, klatawa.
ABSENT — halo mitlite.
ABSOLVE — mamook stoh; mamook mahsh.
ACCEPT — iskum.
ACCIDENT — nika tumtum halo yaka chako kahkwa.
ACCOMPANY — klatawa kunamokst; chako kunamokst.
ACCOMPLISH — mamook.
ACCORDING TO — kopa.
ACCUMULATE — iskum hiyu.
ACCURATE — delate.
ACHIEVE — mamook.
ACKNOWLEDGE — wawa nowitka.
ACORN, ACORNS — kahnaway.
ACQUAINT — mamook kumtux.
ACQUIRE — iskum.
ACROSS — enati; inati.
ACT, ACTION — mamook.
ACTIVE — delate halo lazy.
ADD — mahsh kunamokst.
ADJOIN — wake siah kopa.
ADMIRE — mitlite kloshe tumtum kopa.
ADMONISH — potlatch kloshe wawa.
ADORE — mitlite delate kloshe tumtum kopa; atole.
ADORN — mamook kloshe.
ADRIFT — cultus mitlite kopa chuck.

104

ADULTERATE — mamook mesachie; mahsh mesachie kunamokst.
ADULTERER — man yaka kumtux kapswolla klootchman.
ADULTERESS — klootchman yaka kumtux kapswolla man.
ADVICE, ADVISE — cultus potlatch tumtum.
AFAR — siah.
AFFIRM — wawa delate.
AFFLICT — mamook trouble; mamook sick tumtum.
AFOOT — kopa lepee.
AFRAID — kwass.
AFTER, AFTERWARDS — kimtah.
AFTERNOON — kimtah sitkum sun.
AGAIN — weght.
AGED — oleman.
AGREE — tumtum kunamokst.
AGROUND — kopa illahee.
AGUE — cole sick.
AH! (ADMIRATION) — wah! hah!
AH! (IN PAIN) — anah!
AHEAD — elip.
AID, HELP — elan, elahan.
AID, TO — mamook elan.
ALARM — mamook kwass.
ALDER — isick stick. Literally "paddlewood."
ALIKE — kahkwa.
ALIVE — mitlite wind.
ALL — konaway.
ALMIGHTY, THE — Saghalie Tyee.
ALMOST — wake siah.
ALMS — elan, or elahan.
ALMS, TO GIVE — mamook klahowyum, or klahowya; potlatch dolla.
ALOFT — kopa saghalie.
ALONE — kopet ikt.
ALSO — weght.
ALTER — mamook huloima.
ALTHOUGH — keschi.
ALWAYS — kwonesum.
AM — mitlite is sometimes used; sometimes no word is used.
AMEN — kloshe kahkwa.
AMERICAN — Boston man.
AMID, AMONG — kunamokst; katsuk.
AMOUNT — konaway.
AMUSE — mamook hehe.
AMUSEMENT — hehe.
ANCIENT — hyas ahnkuttie.
AND — pe.
ANGER, ANGRY — solleks.

ANGLER — pish man.
ANNUAL — ikt cole ikt cole.
ANOTHER — huloima.
ANSWER — killapi wawa.
ANTICIPATE — mamook tumtum elip.
ANUS — opoots.
ANXIOUS — hyas ticky.
ANY — klaksta.
APART — ikt yahwa, ikt yahwa.
APPEAL — wawa kopa elip hyas court.
APPEAR — chako kah (nika) nanitch.
APPLE — lapome; apple.
APPLY — (if in words) wawa; (if of things) mahsh.
APPROACH — chako wake siah.
APPROVE — (nika) tumtum kahkwa.
APRON — kissu; kehsu.
ARCTIC — kah delate hiyu cole mitlite.
ARDENT — waum tumtum.
ARGUE — hiyu wawa.
ARGUMENT — mamook hiyu; mamook hyas.
ARISE — mitwhit.
ARITHMETIC — book yaka mamook kumtux nesika kopa kwunnum; mamook tzum.
ARM — lamah.
ARM, TO — iskum musket.
AROUND — wake siah kopa.
AROUSE — mamook get up.
ARREST — mamook haul; mamook kow.
ARRIVE, ARRIVE AT — ko; chako; klap.
ARROW — kalitan; stick kalitan.
AS — kahkwa.
AS IF — kahkwa spose.
ASCEND — klatawa saghalie.
ASH — isick stick.
ASK — wawa.
ASLEEP — moosum.
ASSEMBLE — chako kunamokst.
ASSENT — wawa nowitka.
ASSESS — mamook tzum iktas.
ASSISTANCE — elahan; help.
AT — kopa.
ATTACK — pight elip.
ATTEND — klatawa.
ATTIRE — iktas.
AUDIENCE — hiyu tillikums kopa house.
AUNT — kwalh; papa or mama yaka ats; tant.
AUTUMN — tenas cole illahee.

AVERSE — halo ticky.
AVIDITY — hyas ticky.
AVOID — klatawa kopa huloima ooahut.
AWAKE — halo moosum; halo sleep.
AWAY — siah.
AWE — kwass.
AWL (shoemaker's) — shoes keepwot, or kipuet.
AXE — lahash.
AYE — nowitka.

B

BABY — tenas.
BACK — emeek.
BAD — mesachie; peshak; cultus.
BAD SPIRIT — mesachie tumtum (if in person); mesachie tahmahnawis (if another spirit).
BAG — lesak.
BALL — lebal.
BARGAIN — mahkook; huyhuy.
BARK — stickskin.
BARK (dog's) — kahmooks wawa.
BARLEY — lashey; larch.
BARREL — tamolitsh.
BARTER — huyhuy.
BASIN — ketling.
BASKET — opekwan.
BAT — polaklie kalakala.
BATH — mamook wash.
BATTLE — pight.
BE — sometimes mitlite is used, sometimes no word is used.
BE STILL — kopet wawa.
BEACH — nauits; polallie illahee.
BEADS — kamosuk.
BEAR (black) — itchwoot; chetwoot; itswoot.
BEAR (grizzly) — siam; siam itchwoot.
BEAR, TO — lolo.
BEARD — tupso.
BEARER — man yaka kumtux lolo.
BEAT, TO — kokshut; mamook kokshut.
BEAUTIFUL — kloshe.
BEAVER — eena.
BECALM — halo wind.
BECAUSE — kahkwa; kehwa.
BECOME, TO — chako.
BECOME HARD — chako kull.
BED — bed.

BED QUILT — tzum pasese.
BEEF — itlwillie.
BEFORE — elip.
BEG — skookum wawa.
BEGIN — chee mamook; mamook elip.
BEGONE — klatawa.
BEHAVE — mamook kloshe.
BEHIND — kimtah.
BEHOLD — nah; nanitch.
BELIEVE — iskum wawa; iskum kopa tumtum.
BELL — tintin; dingding; ring the bell, mamook tintin.
BELLE — kloshe tenas klootchman.
BELLY — yakwahtin.
BELOVED — kloshe; kloshe kopa tumtum.
BELOW — keekwullie.
BELT — lasanshel.
BENEATH — keekwullie.
BENEFIT — (v.) mamook kloshe.
BERRIES — olallie; olillie.
BESIDE, BESIDES — kunamokst.
BEST — elip kloshe kopa konoway.
BETTER — elip kloshe.
BETWEEN — kunamokst; katsuk; potsuk.
BEYOND — yahwa.
BIBLE — saghalie tyee yaka book.
BIG — hyas.
BIRD — kalakala; kulakula.
BISCUIT — lebiskwee, or labisquee.
BIT or DIME — bit.
BITE — muckamuck.
BITTER — klikl; klile.
BLACK — klale.
BLACKBERRIES — klale olallie; klikamuks.
BLACKBIRD — pil okchok.
BLACKFISH — klale pish.
BLANKET — pasese.
BLEED — mamook pilpil.
BLESS, TO — wawa kloshe.
BLESSING — kloshe wawa.
BLIND — halo seeowist; halo nanitch.
BLOOD — pilpil.
BLOW, TO — wind chako; hiyu wind.
BLOW OUT — mamook poh.
BLUE (LIGHT) — spooh.
BLUE (DARK) — klale.
BLUNDER, TO — tseepe.

BLUSH — chako pil kopa yaka seeowist.
BOARD — laplash.
BOAST — hyas wawa; skookum wawa.
BOAT — boat.
BOBTAILED — (a bob-tailed horse) siskiyou.
BOIL, TO — liplip; mamook liplip.
BOLD, BOLDNESS — skookum tumtum; halo kwass.
BONE — stone.
BOOK — book.
BOOTS — stick shoes.
BORE, TO — mamook thalwhop; mamook hole.
BORROW, TO — iskum dolla, alki pay.
BOSOM — (female) tatoosh; yahwahtin.
BOSS — tyee.
BOSTON — American.
BOTH — kunamokst; mokst.
BOTTLE — labootai.
BOW — opitlkegh; stick musket.
BOW — (of boat) nose.
BOWELS — kiyah.
BOWL — ooskan; uskan.
BOX — lacaset.
BOX, TO (fight) — mamook pukpuk.
BOY — tenas man.
BRACELET — klikwallie; kweokweo.
BRANCH — tsialits.
BRASS — pil chikamin; klikwallie.
BRAVE — skookum tumtum.
BREAD — lepan; sapolil; piah sapolil (baked bread).
BREAK, TO — kokshut; mamook kokshut; mamook klimmin.
BREAKFAST — muckamuck kopa tenas sun.
BREAST, THE CHEST — emih.
BREASTS — tatoosh.
BREATH — wind.
BREECH CLOUT — opoots sail.
BRIDE — klootchman yaka chee mallie.
BRIDEGROOM — man yaka chee mallie.
BRIDLE — lableed.
BRIGHT — towagh; tewagh.
BRING, TO — lolo; mamook chako; newah.
BRITISH — King Chautsh (George) (kinchautsh).
BROAD — klukulh.
BROKEN LEGGED — kokshut lepee.
BROOK — tenas chuck; tenas cooley chuck.
BROOM — bloom.

BROTHER — kahpho; elip ow (if older than the speaker); kimtah ow (if younger). Male cousins the same.
BROTHER-IN-LAW — ats yaka man; klootchman yaka ow; ekkeh.
BROWN — sitkum klale; tenas klale; klale.
BUCK — man mowitch.
BUCKET — tamolitsh.
BUFFALO — moosmoos; wild moosmoos.
BUILD — mamook house.
BUILDER — laplash man.
BULL — man moosmoos.
BULLET — lebal; kalitan; musket yaka ball.
BUNDLE — kow; iktas.
BURN — mamook piah.
BURST — kokshut.
BURY — mahsh kopa illahee.
BUSHEL (bushel basket) — ikt tamolitsh.
BUT — pe.
BUTCHER — man yaka kumtux mamook memaloose moosmoos.
BUTTER — tatoosh glease; tatoosh lakles.
BUTTONS — chilchil; tsiltsil.
BUY, TO — mahkook.
BY — wake siah kopa; kopa.
BY-AND-BY — winapee; alki.

C

CALF — tenas moosmoos.
CALICO — tzum sail; sail.
CALL, TO — wawa.
CALM — halo wind.
CAMAS — camas, kamass.
CAN — skookum kopa.
CANDLE — lashandel; glease piah.
CANNOT — halo skookum kopa; howkwutl.
CANOE — canim.
CANYON — tanino.
CAP — seahpo.
CAPABLE — skookum kopa; skookum tumtum.
CAPSIZE — killapi; keellapie.
CAPTIVE — elitee.
CAPTURE — mamook kow.
CAR (railroad) — piah chikchik.
CAREFUL — kloshe nanitch.
CARELESS — cultus; halo kloshe nanitch.
CARPENTER — laplash man.
CARRION — humm itlwillie.
CARROT — lacalat.

CARRY, TO — lolo.
CART — chikchik.
CARVE — mamook cut.
CASCADE — tumwata.
CASH — dolla; chikamin.
CASK — tamolitsh.
CAT — pusspuss.
CATARACT — tumwata.
CATCH — iskum; mamook kwutl.
CATTLE — moosmoos.
CAUTIOUS, TO BE — kloshe nanitch.
CEASE — kopet.
CEDAR — canim stick; lametsin stick; kalakwahtee.
CEDAR BARK (inside) — kalakwahtee.
CELESTIAL — kopa saghalie.
CELLAR — ketwilla.
CEMETERY — memaloose illahee.
CENTER — katsuk.
CERTAIN — delate.
CERTAINLY — nowitka.
CHAIN — lashen; chikamin lope.
CHAIR — lashase.
CHANCE — nika tumtum halo yaka chako kahkwa.
CHANGE — huyhuy; mamook huyhuy.
CHANNEL — ooahut.
CHEAP — wake hyas mahkook.
CHEAT, TO — lalah; mamook pelton.
CHEATED, (I am) — nika chako pelton.
CHEEKS — seeowist, capala.
CHEER — hiyu kloshe wawa.
CHEESE — kull tatoosh.
CHICKEN — lapool.
CHIEF — tyee.
CHILD — tenas.
CHILLY — tenas cole.
CHIMNEY — lasheminay.
CHIN — makeson.
CHOOSE — elip ticky.
CHOP, TO — tlkope.
CHRISTMAS — hyas Sunday; klismes.
CIDER — chuck lapome.
CIRCLE — kweokweo.
CITY — skookum town.
CLAM, TO—mamook ona (razor clams); mamook lukutchee, or tukutchee, or tukwitchee (little neck clams); mamook smetocks (the large, round clams of Puget Sound and the northern coasts).

CLAMS — ona; tukutchee; tukwitchee; clams (smetocks the large kind).
CLAY — klimmin illahee.
CLEAN — halo illahee; mamook clean.
CLEAN, TO — mamook clean.
CLEAR — klah.
CLEAR UP, TO — chako klah.
CLERK — tzum man.
CLIMB — klatawa saghalie.
CLOCK — hyas tiktik.
CLOSE — mamook ikpooie.
CLOTH — (cotton or linen) sail or sill; (woolen) pasese.
CLOTHES — iktas.
CLOUDS — smoke; smoke kopa saghalie; cultus smoke.
COAST — illahee wake siah kopa chuck.
COAT — capo; kapo.
COFFEE — kaupy.
COLD — cole; chis.
COLOR — tzum; chym.
COMB — comb.
COMB, TO — mamook comb.
COME, TO — chako; newhah.
COME OUT OF THE WATER — chako klahanie kopa chuck.
COMMAND — law.
COMMAND, TO — mahsh wawa.
COMMANDMENTS — saghalie tyee law.
COMMENCE — mamook begin; chee mamook.
COMMON — kloshe kopa konaway; cultus.
COMMUNION — Jesus yaka muckamuck.
COMPLETE — mamook kopet.
CONCEAL — ipsoot.
CONCEIVE — klap tenas.
CONCEIVE (in mind) — mamook tumtum.
CONCUR — tumtum kahkwa.
CONFESS, TO — yiem; wawa.
CONGREGATE — chako; klatawa kunamokst.
CONJURE, CONJURER — siwash doctin; tahmahnawis man.
CONJURING — tahmahnawis; mamook tahmahnawis.
CONQUER, TO — tolo.
CONSCIENCE — tumtum.
CONSECRATE — potlatch kopa saghalie tyee.
CONTENTED — mitlite kloshe tumtum.
CONVERSATION — CONVERSE — wawa.
COOK — mamook piah; mamook piah muckamuck.
COOKED — chako piah.
COOL, TO — mamook cole.
COPPER — pil chikamin.

COPY — mamook tzum.
CORD — tenas lope; lope.
CORK, TO — ikpooie.
CORN — esalth.
CORRAL — kullah; kullaghan.
CORRECT — delate.
COST (how much) — kunsih dolla?
COTTON, GOODS — sail.
COUGAR — hyas pusspuss.
COUGH, TO COUGH — hohhoh.
COUNSEL — cultus potlatch tumtum.
COUNT — mamook kwunnum; mamook kunsih; mamook tahnim.
COUNTRY — illahee.
COUPLE — mokst.
COURAGE — skookum tumtum.
COUSIN — kahpho.
COVER — mahsh ikta kopa saghalie.
COVET — ticky kapswolla.
COW — klootchman moosmoos.
COWARD — halo skookum tumtum; kwass man.
COYOTE — talapus.
CRABAPPLE — powitsh; siwash apple.
CRACK — tsugh.
CRANBERRY — solemie; swamp olallie; pil olallie.
CRANE — kelok.
CRAZY — pelton.
CREAM — kloshe tatoosh.
CREAM, CREAM-COLORED — leclem.
CREATOR — saghalie tyee.
CREEK — tenas chuck.
CREEK — tenas cooley.
CROOKED — kiwa; tseepe; klooked; wake delate.
CROSS, A — lacloa.
CROW — kahkah.
CROWD — hiyu tillikums.
CRY, TO — cly.
CUP — ooskan; cup; lepot.
CURE — mamook kloshe.
CURED — chako kloshe.
CURLY — hunlkih.
CURRANT — pil olallie; culant.
CURRENCY — pepah dolla.
CURSE — mesachie wawa.
CURSE, TO — wawa mesachie.
CUT, TO — tlkope; mamook cut.

D

DAGGER — opitsah.
DANCE, TO — tanse.
DANGER — mesachie mitlite.
DARK, DARKNESS — polaklie.
DARKEN — mamook polaklie.
DASH, TO — mahsh.
DAUGHTER — tenas klootchman, okustee.
DAWN — delate tenas sun; chee chako light.
DAY — sun.
DAYBREAK — sun chako.
DAYLIGHT — towagh.
DEAD — memaloose; mahsh konaway yaka wind; yaka wind chako halo,
    atimin.
DEAF — ikpooie kwolan; halo kwolan.
DEAFEN — mamook halo kwolan.
DEAF MUTE — halo kwolan halo wawa.
DEAR (expensive) — hyas mahkook.
DEAR (loved) — kloshe.
DEBATE — pight wawa.
DECEIT — kliminawhit wawa.
DECEIVE — wawa kliminawhit mamook lalah.
DECIDE — mamook tumtum; klap tumtum.
DECISION — tumtum.
DECLINE — wawa halo.
DECREASE — chako tenas.
DEED — mamook.
DEEP — klip; hyas keekwullie.
DEER — mowitch.
DEFEAT, TO — tolo.
DEFEND — kloshe nanitch.
DEFER — mamook alki; mamook byby.
DEFORMED — wake delate.
DEITY — saghalie tyee.
DELIGHT — kloshe tumtum.
DELIGHTED — mitlite; chako kloshe tumtum.
DELIRIOUS — huloima latate; kahkwa clazy.
DELUDE — mamook tseepe.
DELUGE — hyas chuck.
DEMAND — wawa; skookum wawa.
DEMON — deaub; mesachie tahmahnawis.
DENTIST — doctin kopa latah.
DENY, DENIAL — wawa halo.
DEPART — klatawa.
DESCENT — klatawa keekwullie.
DESCRIBE — mamook kumtux.

DESERT — illahee kah halo ikta mitlite.
DESERT, TO — kapswolla klatawa; mahsh.
DESIRE — ticky.
DESTROY — mamook halo.
DEVIL — deaub.
DIABOLICAL — kahkwa deaub.
DID — mamook.
DIE — memaloose; mahsh konoway yaka wind.
DIFFERENT, DIFFERENCE — huloima.
DIFFICULT — kull.
DIG — mamook illahee; mamook kokshut illahee.
DIG A HOLE — mamook hole.
DILUTE — mahsh chuck kunamokst.
DIME — bit; ikt bit.
DINE, DINNER — muckamuck kopa sitkum sun.
DIRECT — delate.
DIRECTLY — alki; winapee; tshike.
DIRTY — illahee mitlite; hyas humm.
DISAGREE — halo tumtum kahkwa.
DISAPPEAR — chako halo.
DISAPPOINT — mamook pelton.
DISBELIEVE — halo tumtum kahkwa.
DISCARD, DISCHARGE — mahsh.
DISCOVER — elip nanitch.
DISHES — lasiet, leplah.
DISHONEST — kumtux kapswolla.
DISLIKE — halo ticky.
DISOBEY — halo iskum wawa; mahsh wawa.
DISPLEASURE (expression of) — anah.
DISSENT — huloima tumtum.
DISTANCE (what?) — kunsih siah?
DISTANCE — siah.
DISTRESS — klahowyum tumtum; klahowyum.
DISTRUST — kwass.
DIVE — klatawa keekwullie kopa chuck.
DO, TO — mamook.
DOCTOR — doctin.
DOCTRESS — klootchman doctin.
DODGE — hyak klatawa; klatawa yahwa yahwa.
DOE — klootchman mowitch.
DOG — kahmooks.
DOLLAR — dolla; tahla; chikamin.
DONATION — cultus potlatch.
DOOR — lapote.
DOUBLE — mokst.
DOUBLE (minded) — mokst tumtum.

DOUBT — halo delate kumtux.
DOWN — keekwullie; whim.
DOWN (of a bird) — kalakala tupso.
DOWNCAST — sick tumtum.
DOWN HILL — keekwullie.
DOWNSTREAM — mimie; cooley chuck.
DOXOLOGY — mahsie kopa saghalie tyee.
DOZEN — tahtlum pe mokst.
DRAWERS (underpants) — keekwullie sakoleks.
DREAD — kwass.
DREAM — dleam; nanitch kopa moosum; moosum nanitch.
DRENCH — mahsh kopa chuck.
DRESS — klootchman coat.
DRINK, TO — muckamuck; muckamuck chuck, kaupy; whiskey, etc.
DRINKABLE — kloshe kopa muckamuck.
DRIP — chuck klatawa.
DRIVE — mamook kishkish.
DRIZZLE — tenas snass.
DROWN — memaloose kopa chuck.
DROWSY — ticky sleep.
DRUG — lametsin.
DRUM (Indian) — pompon.
DRUNK — pahtlum.
DRUNKARD — pahtlum man; man kwonesum pahtlum.
DRY, DRYNESS — dly; dely.
DUCK (mallard) — hahthaht.
DUCKING — mahsh kopa chuck; klatawa kopa chuck.
DUG — mamook dig.
DULL — halo tumtum; siah latate.
DUMB — wake wawa; halo wawa.
DURING — kopa.
DUST — polallie; tenas illahee; klimmin klimmin illahee.
DWELL — mitlite.
DYE, TO — mamook tzum.
DYING — wake siah memaloose.

E

EACH — ikt ikt.
EAGER — ticky.
EAGER, TO BE — hyas ticky.
EAGLE — chakchak.
EAR — kwolan.
EARLY — tenas sun.
EARN, TO — tolo.
EARNEST — skookum tumtum.
EARTH — illahee.

EAST — kah sun yaka chako.
EASTER — Paska.
EASY — halo kull.
EAT, TO — muckamuck.
EATABLE — kloshe kopa muckamuck.
EBB TIDE — chuck yaka klatawa.
EDUCATE — mamook kumtux.
EEL (lamprey) — skwakwal.
EFFECTS — iktas.
EFFEMINATE — kahkwa klootchman.
EFFICIENT — skookum; kloshe.
EGG, EGGS — hen olallie.
EIGHT — stotekin; kwinnum pe klone; eight.
EIGHTEEN — tahtlum pe stotekin.
EIGHT HUNDRED — stotekin tukomonuk.
EIGHTY — stotekin tahtlum.
EITHER — OR — klonas klonas.
EJECT — mahsh klahanie.
ELBOW — kimta lamah.
ELDER — elip.
ELDER BROTHER — kaupho.
ELEGANT — hyas kloshe.
ELEVATE — mamook saghalie.
ELK — moolack; mooluk.
ELOPE — kapswolla kopa klootchman.
ELOQUENT — kumtux wawa.
ELSE — huloima.
ELUDE — ipsoot, klatawa.
EMBARK — klatawa kopa canim; boat; ship.
EMBLEM — kahkwa picture.
EMBRACE — iskum kopa lamah.
EMIGRATE — klatawa kopa huloima illahee.
EMOTION — cly tumtum; kahkwa cly.
EMPLOYER — tyee; boss.
EMPTY — halo ikta mitlite.
ENACT — mamook.
ENCIRCLE — ikt yahwa, ikt yahwa, ikt yahwa, pe mamook kow.
ENCLOSE — mamook keekwullie.
ENCLOSURE — kullah.
END — opoots.
ENDEAVOR — ticky mamook.
ENDLESS — kwonesum.
ENDURE — kwonesum mamook; kwonesum mitlite.
ENEMY — solleks tillikum; mesachie tillikum.
ENERGY — skookum mamook.
ENGLAND — King Chautsh Illahee.

ENGLISH, ENGLISHMAN — King Chautsh man; King Chautsh tillikum.
ENGLISH (language) — Boston wawa.
ENGRAVE — mamook tzum.
ENJOY — mitlite kloshe tumtum.
ENLARGE — mamook hyas.
ENOUGH — kopet hiyu; hiyu; kopet.
ENRAGED — solleks.
ENSLAVE — mamook elitee.
ENTER — klatawa keekwullie; klatawa inside.
ENTERTAIN (as a guest) — kloshe nanitch.
ENTIRE — konaway.
ENTRAILS — kiya.
ENTRAP — iskum kopa trap.
ENUMERATE — mamook kunsih; mamook tzum.
EPILEPSY — sick, kahkwa clazy.
EQUAL — kahkwa.
ERECT — mitwhit; delate.
ESCAPE — chako klahanie (for first or second persons); klatawa klahanie
    (for third person); klatawa; klah.
ESCORT, TO — klatawa kunamokst pe kloshe nanitch.
ESTIMATE — tumtum.
ESTIMATE, TO — mamook tumtum.
ETERNAL — kwonesum.
EULOGIZE — wawa kloshe wawa.
EVACUATE — mamook halo; konaway klatawa klahanie.
EVEN — konoway kahkwa; kloshe.
EVENING — tenas polaklie.
EVER, EVERLASTING — kwonesum.
EVERY — konaway.
EVERYWHERE — konaway kah.
EVICT — mahsh klahanie.
EVIL — mesachie.
EWE — klootchman lemooto.
EXACT — delate.
EXAGGERATE — wake siah kliminawhit.
EXALT — mamook saghalie; mamook hyas.
EXALTED — chako saghalie; klatawa saghalie; chako hyas.
EXAMINE — delate nanitch.
EXCEED — chako elip hiyu.
EXCEL — elip kloshe.
EXCELLENT — hyas kloshe.
EXCEPT — kopet.
EXCESS — elip hiyu.
EXCHANGE — huyhuy.
EXCITE — mamook hyas yaka tumtum.
EXCLAIM, EXCLAMATION — skookum wawa; wawa.

EXCLUDE, EXCOMMUNICATE — mahsh klahanie.
EXCUSE — mamook klahowya.
EXECUTE — mamook memaloose.
EXERCISE, EXERT — mamook.
EXERT — hiyu mamook.
EXHALE — mahsh wind.
EXHAUST — mamook till.
EXHAUSTED — chako delate till; wake siah memaloose kopa till.
EXHORT — skookum wawa; wawa skookum.
EXILE, TO — mahsh.
EXIST — mitlite.
EXPATRIATE — mahsh klahanie kopa yaka illahee.
EXPEDITE — mamook hyak.
EXPEL — mahsh.
EXPEND — pay; potlatch.
EXPERT — delate yaka kumtux.
EXPIRE — memaloose; mahsh konaway yaka wind.
EXPLAIN — mamook kumtux.
EXPLORE — klatawa pe nanitch.
EXQUISITE — delate kloshe.
EXTEND — mamook hyas.
EXTENDED — chako hyas.
EXTENSIVE — hyas.
EXTERIOR — klahanie.
EXTERMINATE, EXTINGUISH — mamook halo; mahsh.
EXTRAORDINARY — hyas huloima.
EXTRAVAGANT — cultus mahkook iktas.
EYE, EYES, EYEBALL — seeowist.
EYELASH — skin kopa seeowist.
EYEWATER — lametsin kopa seeowist.
EYEWITNESS — man yaka delate nanitch.

F

FABLE — wake delate wawa.
FABRIC — iktas.
FACE — seeowist.
FACILITY — halo kull.
FACT — delate wawa.
FADE — chako spooh.
FADED — spooh.
FAGGED — chako till.
FAIR — kloshe.
FALL — fall down; mamook whim.
FALLEN — whim.
FALSE, FALSEHOOD — kliminawhit; tseepe.
FAME — hyas nem.

FAMILY — tillikums.
FAMINE — halo muckamuck.
FAMISH — wake siah memaloose kopa olo.
FAR — siah.
FARM — illahee.
FARTHER — elip siah.
FARTHEST — elip siah kopa konaway.
FAST (tight) — kwutl; hyas kull.
FAST (quick) — hyak.
FASTEN — mamook kow.
FAT — glease.
FATHER — papa.
FATHOM — itlan.
FATIGUE — till.
FATTEN — mamook glease.
FAULT — wake delate mamook.
FAVOR — kloshe tumtum.
FAWN — tenas mowitch; mowitch yaka tenas.
FEAR, FEARFUL — kwass.
FEARLESS — halo kwass.
FEAST — muckamuck; hiyu muckamuck.
FEATHER — kalakala tupso.
FEEBLE — wake skookum; halo skookum.
FEED — potlatch muckamuck.
FEEL (with hand) — kumtux kopa lamah.
FEEL (with heart) — sick tumtum.
FEET — lepee.
FELL, TO (as a tree) — mamook whim.
FELLOW — tillikum.
FEMALE — klootchman.
FERMENT — kahkwa liplip; chako waum.
FENCE — kullah; kullahan; pence.
FEROCIOUS — hyas ticky pight; delate kumtux pight.
FERVENT, FERVOR — waum tumtum.
FESTER — chako sick pe chako hyas.
FESTIVAL — hyas kloshe time; hiyu muckamuck.
FETCH — lolo; mamook chako.
FEVER — waum sick.
FEVER AND AGUE — waum sick, cole sick.
FEW — wake hiyu; tenas.
FIB — kliminawhit.
FICTION — wake delate wawa.
FIELD — illahee.
FIEND — mesachie tahmahnawis.
FIERCE — hyas ticky pight.
FIFTEEN — tahtlum pe kwinnum.

FIFTY — kwinnum tahtlum.
FIGHT, TO — mamook solleks; pight; kahdena.
FIGHT (with fists) — mamook pukpuk.
FIGURED (as calico) — tzum.
FILE — laleem.
FILL, TO — mamook pahtl.
FILTHY — mesachie; humm; cultus.
FIN — pish yaka lamah.
FIND, TO — klap.
FINE — kloshe.
FINE, TO — mamook fine.
FINGER — ledoo.
FINGER RING — kweokweo.
FINISH — mamook kopet.
FIR — moola stick.
FIRE — piah; olapitski.
FIREPLACE — kah piah mitlite.
FIRM — skookum.
FIRST — elip.
FIRST BORN — elip tenas.
FISH — pish.
FISHERMAN — pishman.
FISHERY — kah pish mitlite; kah iskum pish.
FISHHOOK — pishhook; ikik.
FISHLINE — pish lope.
FISHROD — pish stick.
FISHY — kahkwa pish.
FISTS — lamah kahkwa.
FIT — kahkwa clazy.
FIVE — kwinnum.
FIVE HUNDRED — kwinnum tukamonuk.
FIX — mamook kloshe.
FLAG — sail; flag; hyas Sunday sail.
FLEA — sopena inapoo; chotub.
FLEE — klatawa.
FLESH — itlwillie; meat.
FLIES — tenas kalakala; lemosh.
FLIMSY — pewhattie; wake skookum.
FLING — mahsh.
FLINT — kilitsut.
FLOAT — mitlite saghalie kopa chuck.
FLOCK — hiyu sheep; kalakala.
FLOOD — hiyu chuck.
FLOUNDER (fish) — tpishkuks.
FLOUR — sapolil; klimmin sapolil.
FLOW — klatawa.

FLOWER, FLOWERS — kloshe tupso.
FLUID — kahkwa chuck.
FLY, TO — mamook fly; kawak.
FOAL, A — tenas kuitan.
FOAL (to be with) — klootchman kuitan yaka mitlite tenas.
FOG — smoke; cultus smoke.
FOLD, SHEEPFOLD — lemooto house.
FOLKS — tillikums.
FOLLOW — klatawa kimtah.
FOLLY — kahkwa pelton.
FOOD — muckamuck.
FOOL — pelton.
FOOLISH, FOOLHARDY — kahkwa pelton.
FOOT — lepee.
FOOTSTEPS, FOOTPRINT — kah lepee mitlite.
FOR — kopa.
FORAGE, GRASS LAND — tupso illahee.
FORBEAR — kopet.
FORBID — wawa kloshe kopet.
FORD — kah kloshe nesika klatawa enati kopa chuck.
FOREFATHER — ahnkuttie papa.
FOREIGN — huloima.
FOREIGNER — huloima tillikum.
FORENOON — elip sitkum sun.
FOREST — kah hiyu stick mitlite.
FORETELL — wawa elip.
FOREVER — kwonesum.
FORGET, TO — mahlie; mahsh tumtum; kopet kumtux.
FORGIVE — mamook klahowya.
FORK (hayfork) — lapushet.
FORKS (of a river or road) — lapush mox.
FORMER — elip.
FORMERLY — ahnkuttie.
FORSAKE — mahsh.
FORTNIGHT — mokst Sunday.
FORTUNATE — kloshe.
FORTY — lakit tahtlum.
FOR WHAT — pe kahta.
FOWL — lapool.
FOUND — klap.
FOUR — lakit; lokit.
FOURTEEN — tahtlum pe lakit.
FOUR HUNDRED — lakit tukamonuk.
FOWL — lapool.
FOX — talapus; hyas opoots talapus.
FRAIL — wake skookum.

FRANCE — Pasiooks illahee.
FRATERNAL — kahkwa ow.
FREE — halo elitee.
FREEZE, FREEZING — hyas cole; shelipo.
FRENCH, FRENCHMAN — Pasiooks.
FREQUENTLY — hiyu times.
FRESH — chee.
FRET — tenas solleks.
FRIDAY — kwinnum sun.
FRIEND — sikhs; six.
FRIENDLY — kloshe tumtum; kahkwa tillikum.
FRIENDLESS — halo tillikum.
FRIGHTEN — mamook kwass.
FRIGHTENED — chako kwass.
FRINGE — tupso.
FROG — shwahkuk; wakik.
FROLIC — hehe.
FROLICSOME — pahtl kopa hehe.
FROM — kopa.
FROWN — kahkwa solleks.
FRY, TO — mamook piah; mamook cook; mamook lapoel.
FRYING PAN — lapoel.
FUEL — piah stick.
FULL — pahtl.
FUN — hehe.
FUND — chikamin: dolla.
FUNERAL — lolo; mahsh memaloose tillikum kopa memaloose illahee.
FUR — eena tupso.
FURNITURE — iktas.
FURTHERMOST, FURTHEST — elip siah kopa konaway.
FUTILE — cultus.
FUTURE — alki; by-by; winapee.

G

GAB, GABBLE — wawa.
GAIN — tolo.
GALE — skookum wind.
GALLOP, TO — kwalalkwalal; hyak klatawa.
GAMBLE — gamble; mamook gamble; mamook itlokum; hehe lamah (with disks).
GAME — hehe.
GARDEN — kloshe illahee.
GARDEN, TO — mamook kloshe illahee.
GARMENTS — iktas.
GAS — kahkwa wind.
GASH, TO — mamook cut; mamook kokshut.

GASP — hyas kull spose yaka iskum yaka wind; wake siah lost yaka wind.
GATHER — iskum; hokumelh.
GAY — kloshe; hehe.
GAZE — skookum nanitch.
GENDER — (is distinguished by prefixing the word man for male, and klootchman for female.)
GENERAL — hyas tyee.
GENEROUS — kloshe kopa cultus potlatch.
GENTLE — halo wind.
GENUINE — delate.
GET, TO — iskum.
GET OUT — klatawa; mahsh.
GET UP — mamook getup; getup.
GHOST — tahmahnawis; skookum.
GIANT — delate hyas man.
GIFT — cultus potlatch.
GIGGLE — hehe.
GILT — kahkwa pil chikamin.
GIRL — tenas klootchman.
GIRLISH — kahkwa tenas klootchman.
GIVE, TO — potlatch.
GLAD — kwan; yotl tumtum.
GLADNESS — ualtee.
GLARE — skookum light.
GLASS — shelokum.
GLEAM — tenas light.
GLEE — hehe.
GLOOM — polaklie.
GLOOMY — kahkwa polaklie (like night).
GLORIOUS — hyas kloshe.
GLORY — hyas kloshe nem.
GNATS — dago.
GNAW — muckamuck; muckamuck kahkwa eena.
GO, TO — klatawa.
GOAD — moosmoos stick.
GOBLIN — tahmahnawis; tsiatko.
GOD — Saghalie Tyee.
GODLESS — halo ticky Saghalie Tyee.
GODLIKE, GODLY — kahkwa Saghalie Tyee.
GOLD — pil chikamin.
GOLDEN — kahkwa pil chikamin.
GOOD — kloshe.
GOOD-BYE — klahowya.
GOOD SPIRIT — kloshe tahmahnawis.
GOODS — iktas.
GOOSE — kalakala.

GORE — pilpil.
GORE, TO — mamook kokshut pe pilpil yaka chako.
GOSPEL — Saghalie Tyee yaka wawa. (God, His word.)
GOVERN — mamook tyee.
GOVERNOR — tyee.
GRACEFUL — kloshe.
GRADUATE, TO — kopet kopa school.
GRAIN — sapolil.
GRAND — hyas kloshe.
GRANDCHILD — tenas yaka tenas.
GRANDDAUGHTER — tenas yaka tenas klootchman.
GRANDFATHER — papa yaka papa (papa of his papa); chope.
GRANDMOTHER — mama yaka mama; chitsh.
GRANDSON — tenas yaka tenas man (son of his son).
GRANT — potlatch.
GRASS — tupso; tupso kopa illahee.
GRASSHOPPER — tlaktlak.
GRATEFUL — mahsie tumtum.
GRATEFUL, TO BE — wawa mahsie.
GRAVE — memaloose illahee.
GRAVESTONE — stone kopa memaloose illahee.
GRAZE — muckamuck tupso.
GREASE — glease.
GREASY — kahkwa glease.
GREAT — hyas.
GREEDY — ticky konaway; hyas ticky.
GREEN — pechugh; (pale green) kawkawak.
GREET — wawa.
GREY — gley.
GRIEF — cly tumtum.
GRIND (as flour) — mamook sapolil; mamook klimmin-klimmin; (as ax) mamook sharp; mamook kloshe.
GRIT — tenas stone; kahkwa stone.
GRIZZLY (bear) — siam; siam itswoot.
GROG — lumpechuck.
GROUND — illahee.
GROUSE — glouse; siwash chicken; siwash lapool.
GROW — chako hyas.
GROWL, GRUMBLE — solleks wawa.
GRUMBLE — sollex wawa.
GRUNT — wawa kahkwa cosho.
GUARD — kloshe nanitch.
GUARDIAN — man yaka kloshe nanitch tenas.
GUARD HOUSE — skookum house.
GUESS — mika tumtum; guess.
GUILT — mesachie.

GUM — lagome.
GUN — musket; sukwalwal.
GUNPOWDER — polallie.
GYPSY — huloima tillikum.

H

HA — nah.
HAIL — cole snass.
HAIR — tupso; tupso kopa latate; yakso.
HAIR BRUSH — tupso bloom.
HALF — sitkum.
HALF-BREED — sitkum siwash; sitkum Boston.
HALIBUT — pows.
HALLOO — nah.
HALT — kopet klatawa; kopet cooley.
HAM — cosho; dly cosho.
HAMMER — lemahto.
HAND — lamah.
HAND (right) — kloshe lamah.
HAND (game of) — itlokum.
HANDCUFF — chickamin kopa mamook kow lamah.
HANDKERCHIEF — hakatshum.
HANDSOME — hyas kloshe.
HANG — memaloose kopa lope kopa yaka neck. (Died with rope around his
    neck.)
HAPPY — kloshe tumtum; yotl tumtum.
HARANGUE — skookum wawa.
HARD — kull.
HARDEN — mamook kull.
HARE — kwitshadie.
HARK — nah; nanitch.
HARLOT — mesachie klootchman.
HARM — mesachie.
HARM, TO — mamook mesachie.
HARROW, TO — mamook comb illahee.
HARVEST — iskum sapolil.
HASTEN — hyak.
HAT — seahpo.
HATCH — chicken chako kopa eggs; tenas lapool chee chako.
HATCHET — tenas lahash.
HAUL — haul.
HAUL, WITH WAGON — lolo kopa chikchik.
HAVE — mitlite.
HAWK — hawk; shakshak.
HAY — hay; dly tupso.
HAZEL NUTS — tukwilla.

HE, HIS — yaka.
HEAD — latate.
HEADACHE — sick kopa latate.
HEADWIND — cultus wind.
HEAL — mamook kloshe.
HEALED — chako kloshe.
HEALTHY — halo sick.
HEAP — hiyu.
HEAR — kumtux kopa kwolan.
HEARSAY — cultus kumtux kopa kwolan.
HEART — tumtum.
HEARTACHE — sick tumtum.
HEAT — waum.
HEAVEN — Saghalie Tyee yaka illahee; koosah; saghalie illahee.
HEAVY — till.
HEED (take) — kloshe nanitch.
HEIRS — yaka tenas pe yaka klootchman.
HELL — hyas piah; deaub yaka illahee; keekwullie illahee.
HELM — ludda.
HELP, TO — mamook elan; mamook help.
HEN — klootchman chicken.
HENCE — kahkwa.
HER — yaka.
HERB — lametsin; tupso.
HERD — hiyu moosmoos.
HERE — yukwa; how nah.
HERMAPHRODITE — Burdash.
HERRING — tenas pish; oolchus.
HERS — yaka.
HERSELF — yaka self.
HEW (to cut or chop) — Tlkope.
HEY — nah.
HIDE, TO — ipsoot.
HIDE OR PELT — skin.
HIGH — saghalie; long; high.
HIGHWAY — ooahut.
HILARITY — hiyu hehe.
HILL — tenas saghalie illahee.
HIM — yaka.
HIMSELF — yaka self.
HINDER — wake siah mamook stop.
HIRE — potlatch mamook.
HIRED — iskum mamook.
HIS — yaka.
HIT, TO — mamook kokshut; kwult.
HIT, TO BE — chako kokshut.

HITCH — mamook kow.
HITHER — yukwa; newhah.
HO — nah.
HOARSE — cole sick wawa.
HOARY — t'kope.
HOE — lapeosh.
HOG — cosho.
HOGGISH — kahkwa cosho.
HOLD — iskum; halo mahsh.
HOLD ON — kloshe mitlite; kloshe wait.
HOLE — klawhop.
HOLIDAY — hyas Sunday; Sunday.
HOLY — kahkwa Saghalie Tyee.
HOLLOW — halo ikta mitlite.
HOME — nika house; illahee.
HONEST — wake kapswolla; halo kumtux kapswolla.
HONEY — honey; kahkwa shugah.
HONOR — kloshe nem.
HOOF — kuitan lepee.
HOP — sopena.
HOPE — ticky kahkwa.
HOPEFUL — halo kwass.
HOPS — tlanemas.
HORN — stone; bone.
HORRIBLE, HORRID — hyas mesachie.
HORROR — hyas kwass.
HORSE — kuitan.
HORSEBACK — kopa kuitan.
HORSEHAIR — kuitan tupso.
HORSE RACE — cooley kuitan.
HORSESHOES — kuitan shoes; chikamin shoes.
HOSE — stocken.
HOSPITABLE — kloshe.
HOSTILE — solleks.
HOT — hyas waum.
HOUR — tintin — adding the number, as klone tintin, three o'clock, etc.
HOUSE — house.
HOW — kahta?
HOW ARE YOU? — klahowya?
HOWL — kahmooks yaka wawa.
HOW LARGE? — kunsih hyas?
HOW MANY? — kunsih?
HUCKLEBERRIES — shot olallie.
HUMAN — kahkwa man.
HUMBLE — halo ploud.
HUMOROUS — hehe.

HUNDRED — tukamonuk.
HUNGRY — olo.
HUNT — mamook hunt.
HURL — mahsh.
HURRY — hyak ; howh.
HURT — kokshut.
HURT, TO — chako kokshut.
HURT ONE'S FEELINGS — mamook sick tumtum.
HUSBAND (MY) — nika man.
HUSH — kopet wawa; kopet noise.
HUT — tenas house.

I

I — nika.
ICE — cole chuck.
IDEA — tumtum.
IDENTICAL — delate kahkwa.
IDIOT — pelton man.
IDLE — cultus mitlite.
IF — spose.
IGNITE — mamook piah.
IGNORANT — halo kumtux; blind kopa tumtum.
ILL; ILLNESS — sick.
ILLTREAT — mamook mesachie; mamook kahta.
IMBECILE — wake skookum latate.
IMBIBE — muckamuck.
IMITATE — mamook kahkwa.
IMITATION — kahkwa mamook.
IMMATERIAL — cultus.
IMMEASURABLE — halo kumtux kunsih hyas.
IMMENSE — delate hyas.
IMMIGRATE — chako kopa ikt illahee.
IMMODEST, IMMORAL — mesachie.
IMPATIENCE — halo ticky mitlite.
IMPERFECT — wake delate.
IMPOSSIBLE — wake skookum kopa.
IMPROBABLE — tumtum yaka halo kahkwa.
IMPROPER — wake kloshe.
IMPROVE — chako tenas kloshe.
IN — kopa.
INABILITY — wake skookum kopa; howkwutl.
INASMUCH — kahkwa.
INCITE — mamook waum yaka tumtum.
INCOMPLETE — wake yaka kopet.
INDEED — nowitka.
INDEPENDENT (he is) — cultus kopa (yaka) kopa huloima tillikums.
INDIAN — siwash.

INDIFFERENT (I am) — cultus kopa nika.
INDOMITABLE — skookum tumtum.
INDUCE (him) — mamook haul yaka tumtum.
INDULGE — iskum.
INDUSTRIOUS — kwonesum mamook.
INEBRIATE — man yaka kwonesum pahtlum; man yaka kwonesum mucka-
muck whiskey.
INFANT — tenas; chee tenas.
INFIRM, SICK — wake skookum.
INK — klale chuck kopa mamook tzum.
INQUIRE — wawa; ask; ticky kumtux.
INSHORE — mahtwillie.
INSIDE — keekwullie.
INSPIRE — mamook waum yaka tumtum.
INSTANTLY — hyak.
INSUFFICIENT — wake hiyu.
INSULT — solleks wawa.
INTEND (I) — nika tumtum.
INTENTION — tumtum.
INTERCEDE (you for me) — kloshe mika potlatch nika wawa kopa yaka.
INTERPRET — mamook kumtux huloima wawa.
INVISIBLE (to you) — wake kahta nanitch.
INTERVAL — tenas laly.
INTIMATE — kloshe.
INWARD — keekwullie.
IRON — chikamin.
IRRESOLUTE — wake skookum tumtum.
IRRIGATE — mamook cooley chuck.
IS — "mitlite" is sometimes used and sometimes no word is used.
ISLAND — tenas illahee.
IT — yaka.
ITCH — tlihtlih.
ITS — yaka.
ITSELF — yaka self.
IVY — stick kahkwa lope.

J

JABBER — cultus wawa.
JACKET — yotskut capo.
JEALOUS — sick tumtum.
JEHOVAH — Saghalie Tyee.
JERK — hyas mamook haul. (Quick make haul).
JERKED BEEF — moosmoos itlwillie chako dly.
JEST — cultus wawa.
JESUS — Saghalie Tyee yaka tenas (son of God).
JOB — mamook.

JOIN — chako kunamokst.
JOKE — cultus wawa.
JOKE, TO — mamook hehe.
JOLLY — hehe tumtum.
JOURNEY — cooley.
JOY, JOYFUL — yotl tumtum.
JUDGE — tyee kopa court.
JUG — stone labootai.
JUICE — olallie chuck.
JUMP, TO — sopena.
JUST — delate. Just a little, delate tenas.

K

KAMASS ROOT—See camas.
KENNEL — kahmooks house.
KETTLE — ketling.
KEY — lekleh.
KICK, TO — mamook kokshut; chukkin.
KILL — mamook memaloose.
KIN — tillikum.
KIND — kloshe.
KINDRED — tillikum.
KISS — bebe.
KITTEN — tenas pusspuss.
KNEAD — mamook lepan.
KNEE — tahness.
KNEEL — mamook kahkwa (showing how).
KNIFE — opitsah.
KNIT — mamook stocken.
KNOCK, TO — koko; mamook kokshut; mamook kahkwa (showing how).
KNOT (of tree) — lamah; lamah kopa stick.
KNOTTED (curled) — hunlkih.
KNOW, TO; KNOWLEDGE — kumtux.
KNUCKLE — yukwa kopa lamah (point to it).

L

LABOR — mamook.
LACK — wake hiyu.
LAD — tenas man.
LADY — klootchman.
LAKE — tsalil.
LAMB — tenas sheep; tenas lemooto; sheep yaka tenas.
LAME — klook teahwit; sick kopa lepee.
LAMENT — cly tumtum.
LAMP — lalamp.
LAND — illahee.

LANDLORD — tyee.
LAND OTTER — nenamooks.
LANE — ooahut.
LANGUAGE — lalang.
LARCENY — kapswolla.
LARD — cosho glease.
LARGE — hyas.
LARK — tenas kalakala.
LAST — delate kimtah; kimtah kopa konaway.
LATELY — chee; tenas ahnkuttie.
LAUGH — hehe; mamook hehe.
LAUGHTER — hehe.
LAUNCH — mahsh boat; ship kopa chuck.
LAWN — kloshe tupso illahee.
LAY — mahsh.
LAZY — lazy.
LEAD (bullet) — kalitan.
LEAD, TO — mamook cooley.
LEADER — tyee.
LEAF, LEAVES — tupso.
LEAN — halo glease.
LEAN, TO — lagh.
LEAP, TO — sopena.
LEARN — iskum kumtux; kumtux.
LEARNED — kumtux hiyu.
LEAST — elip tenas kopa konaway.
LEATHER — skin; dly skin.
LEAVE, TO — mahsh; klatawa.
LEAVE OFF, TO — kopet.
LECTURE — wawa.
LEG — teahwit; lepee.
LEGAL — kloshe kopa law.
LEGEND — wawa; wake delate wawa.
LEGGINGS — mitass.
LEGISLATURE — tyee man klaska mamook law.
LEND, TO — ayahwhul; ticky owe.
LENGTH — yotlkut.
LESS — tenas.
LETTER — pepah.
LEVEL — konaway kahkwa; flat.
LIAR — yaka kumtux wawa kliminawhit.
LIBERAL — kloshe kopa cultus potlatch.
LICK, TO — klakwun.
LICE — inapoo.
LIE — kliminawhit wawa; kliminawhit.
LIE, TO — wawa kliminawhit; kliminawhit.

LIE DOWN — mitlite.
LIGHT (not heavy) — halo till; wake till.
LIGHT (not dark) — halo polaklie.
LIGHT, DAYLIGHT — twah.
LIGHTNING — saghalie piah.
LIKE (similar) — kahkwa.
LIKE (want) — ticky.
LIMB — (of person) lamah; (of tree) stick yaka lamah.
LINGER — mitlite; halo chako.
LINGUIST — yaka kumtux hiyu lalang.
LINIMENT — lametsin kopa skin.
LIPS — lapush (point to them).
LISP — wake delate wawa.
LISTEN — hah; nanitch.
LITTLE — tenas.
LIVE — halo memaloose.
LIVE, TO — mitlite.
LIVER — haslitch.
LODGE — tenas house; siwash house.
LOFTY — saghalie.
LOGGING CAMP — stick house.
LONELY — kopet ikt.
LONG — yotlkut.
LONG AGO — ahnkuttie.
LOOK, TO — nanitch; nah.
LOOK AROUND — cultus nanitch.
LOOK HERE! — nah!
LOOK OUT! — kloshe nanitch!
LOOKING GLASS — shelokum.
LOOSE — stoh; mahsh kow.
LOUD — skookum latlah.
LOUSE — inapoo.
LOSE THE WAY — tsolo; tseepe ooahut.
LOVE, TO — ticky.
LOW — keekwullie.
LOWER — elip keekwullie.
LOWER, TO — mamook keekwullie.
LOWLY — halo ploud tumtum.
LUKEWARM (indifferent) — tenas lazy; (tepid) tenas waum.
LUG — lolo.
LUMBER — laplash.
LUNCH — muckamuck.

M

MAD — solleks.
MADAM — klootchman.

MAGIC — tahmahnawis.
MAGISTRATE — tyee.
MAGNIFICENT — delate hyas kloshe.
MAIZE — corn; esalth.
MAJORITY — elip hiyu.
MAKE, TO — mamook.
MALE — man.
MALICE — mesachie tumtum; solleks.
MALLARD DUCK — hahthaht.
MAMMA — mama.
MAN — man.
MANAGE — tolo; mamook.
MANE — kuitan yakso.
MANGLE — hiyu mamook cut.
MANKIND — konaway tillikums.
MANLY — kahkwa man.
MANNER — kahkwa kwonesum yaka mamook.
MANSION — hyas house.
MANY — hiyu.
MAPLE — isick stick.
MARBLE — kloshe stone.
MARE — klootchman kuitan.
MARK — tzum.
MARK, TO — mamook tzum.
MARKET — mahkook house.
MARRIAGE, MARRY — mallie.
MARROW — glease mitlite kopa bone.
MASK — stick seeowist.
MASSACRE, TO — cultus mamook memaloose.
MASS (ceremony of) — lamesse.
MAST — ship stick.
MASTER — tyee.
MAT — kliskwiss.
MATERNAL — kahkwa mama.
MATRIMONY — mallie.
MATRON — tyee klootchman.
MATTOCK — lapeosh.
MATURE — piah.
MAXIMUM — elip hiyu kopa konaway.
MAYOR — tyee kopa town.
ME — nika.
MEADOW — tupso, illahee.
MEAL (flour) — sapolil.
MEAL — muckamuck.
MEAN — delate cultus; wake kloshe.
MEASURE, TO — tahnim; mamook measure.

MEAT — itlwillie; meat.
MEDICINE — lametsin.
MEDICINE MAN (Indian) — keelally.
MEDITATE — mamook tumtum.
MEEK — kloshe; halo solleks; kwan.
MEET — chako kunamokst.
MELANCHOLY — sick tumtum.
MELLOW — piah.
MELT — chako chuck; chako kahkwa chuck; chako klimmin.
MEMORY — tumtum.
MEND, TO — mamook tupshin.
MENSTRUATE — mahsh pilpil.
MENTAL — kopa tumtum.
MENTION — wawa.
MERCHANDISE — iktas.
MERCHANT — mahkook man.
MERCHANTABLE — kloshe kopa mahkook.
MERCIFUL, TO BE — mamook klahowya.
MERRY — kwan.
MESSAGE (verbal) — wawa.
MESSAGE (written) — pepah.
METAL, METALLIC — chikamin; kahkwa chikamin.
METROPOLIS — tyee town.
MIDDAY — sitkum sun.
MIDDLE, THE — katsuk; sitkum.
MIDNIGHT — sitkum polaklie.
MIDSUMMER — sitkum kopa waum illahee.
MIDST — kunamokst.
MIGHT (strength) — skookum.
MIGRATE — klatawa.
MILD — kloshe.
MILK — tatoosh.
MILKMAN — tatoosh man.
MILKY — kahkwa tatoosh.
MILL — moola.
MILLER — moola man.
MIMIC — mamook kahkwa.
MIND, THE — tumtum.
MINE — illahee kah chikamin mitlite.
MINGLE — klatawa kunamokst; mamook kunamokst; mahsh kunamokst.
MINISTER — leplet.
MINNOW — tenas pish.
MINOR — tenas; elip tenas.
MIRACLE — huloima mamook.
MIRROR — shelokum.
MIRTH — hehe.

MISCHIEF — cultus mamook.
MISCONDUCT — mesachie mamook.
MISPRONOUNCE — halo delate wawa; tseepe wawa; huloima wawa.
MISS, TO — tseepe.
MISSIONARY — leplet.
MISTAKE — tseepe mamook.
MISTAKE, TO — mamook tseepe.
MISTY — tenas snass.
MISUNDERSTAND — halo kumtux.
MITE (a little) — tenas.
MIX — mamook kunamokst; mamook klimmin.
MOAN — cly.
MOB — sollex tillikum.
MOCCASINS — skin-shoes.
MOCK — mamook shem; mamook hehe.
MODERATE — wake hyak.
MODEST — kloshe.
MOISTURE — tenas chuck.
MOLASSES — melass; silup; molassis.
MOLE — skad.
MONDAY — ikt sun.
MONEY — chikamin; dolla.
MONTH — moon.
MONTHLY — ikt moon — ikt moon.
MOON — moon.
MOONLIGHT, MOONSHINE — moon yaka light.
MOOSE — ulchey; hyas mowitch.
MORAL (upright) — kloshe.
MORE — weght; elip hiyu.
MORNING — tenas sun.
MOSS — tupso.
MOSQUITO — melakwa; dago.
MOST — elip hiyu kopa konaway.
MOTHER — mama; naha.
MOTHERLESS — halo mama.
MOTHERLY — kahkwa mama.
MOTTLED (dappled) — lekye.
MOUNTAIN — stone illahee; lamontay.
MOURN — cly tumtum.
MOUSE — hoolhool; cultus hoolhool.
MOUTH — lapush; laboos.
MOVE — tenas mahsh; mamook move.
MOW — mamook cut; mamook tlkope.
MOWER — machine kopa mamook cut hay.
MUCH — hiyu.
MUD — mud; klimmin illahee.

MUDDY (muddy water) — illahee mitlite kopa chuck (land is with water).
MUDDY (muddy ground) — chuck mitlite kopa illahee (water is with land).
MULE — lemel; lemool.
MULISH — kahkwa lemool.
MUM — halo wawa.
MURDER — mamook memaloose.
MURMUR — tenas pight wawa.
MURMUR, TO — potlatch tenas pight wawa.
MUSE, TO — mamook tumtum.
MUSIC — tintin.
MUSICIAN — man yaka kumtux tintin.
MUSICAL INSTRUMENT — tintin.
MUSKET — musket.
MUSKRAT — emintepu.
MUSSELS — toluks.
MUSTARD — piah tupso.
MUTE — halo wawa.
MUTTER — wawa.
MUTTON — sheep yaka meat; lemooto yaka itlwillie.
MY, MINE — nika.
MYSELF — nika self.
MYSTERY — hyas huloima.

N

NAB — iskum.
NAIL — lekloo.
NAILS (finger nails and toenails) — towah.
NAKED — halo ikta mitlite.
NAME — nem; yahhul.
NAMELESS — halo nem.
NAP — tenas sleep; tenas moosum.
NARROW — halo wide.
NASTY — wake kloshe; mesachie.
NATION — tillikum.
NATIVE — delate yaka illahee.
NAVEL — tentome.
NAVIGATE — klatawa kopa chuck.
NAY — wake; halo.
NEAR — wake siah.
NEAT — kloshe.
NECK — lecoo.
NEED — hyas ticky.
NEEDY — klahowyum.
NEEDLE — keepwot; tupshin.
NEGATIVE — halo; wake.
NEGLECT — halo kloshe nanitch.

NEIGHBORHOOD — tillikum mitlite wake siah.
NEPHEW — ack; kaupho (or ow or ats) yaka tenas man.
NERVE OR NERVES — tlepait.
NEST — kalakala house.
NEVER — wake kunsih.
NEW — chee.
NEWS — chee wawa.
NICE — kloshe.
NIECE — kaupho (or ow or ats) yaka tenas klootchman.
NIGH — wake siah.
NIGHT — polaklie.
NINE — kwaist; kweest.
NINETEEN — tahtlum pe kweest.
NINETY — kweest tahtlum.
NO, NOT — halo; wake.
NOBODY — wake tillikum.
NOD — kahkwa sleep; moosum; wake siah sleep; moosum.
NOISE — noise; latlah.
NOISELESS — halo noise.
NOISY — hiyu noise.
NONE — halo; wake.
NONSENSE — cultus wawa.
NOON — sitkum sun.
NORTH — kah cole chako.
NOSE — nose; emeets.
NOT — halo; wake.
NOTHING — halo ikta.
NOTWITHSTANDING — keschi.
NOURISH — potlatch muckamuck.
NOW — witka.
NOWHERE — halo kah.
NOZZLE — nose.
NUMB — kahkwa memaloose.
NUMBER — klonas kunsih.
NUMERALS—
  1. ikt; icht.
  2. mokst, moxt.
  3. klone.
  4. lakit; lokit.
  5. kwinnum.
  6. taghum; tughum.
  7. sinamokst; sinamoxt.
  8. stotekin.
  9. kwaist; kweest.
  10. tahtlum.
  11. tahtlum pe ikt.

20. mokst tahtlum.
100. ikt tukamonuk; icht tukamonuk; tahtlum-tahtlum—ten tens.
NURSE — klootchman; man yaka kloshe nanitch.
NURSE, TO — kloshe nanitch.
NUTRIMENT — muckamuck.
NUTS — tukwilla.

O

OAK — kull stick.
OAR — lalahm.
OATS — lawen; laween.
OBEDIENCE, OBEDIENT, OBEY — iskum wawa; mamook kahkwa yaka wawa.
OBJECT — wawa halo.
OBLIGE (a favor) — mamook help.
OBSCENE — mesachie.
OBSCURE — halo delate kumtux.
OBSERVE — nanitch.
OBTAIN — iskum.
OCEAN — hyas salt chuck.
OCHRE — kawkawak illahee.
ODD — huloima.
ODOR — humm.
OFF — klak.
OFFEND — mamook solleks; mamook kahta.
OFFER — ticky potlatch.
OFFICER — tyee.
OFF SHORE — mahtlinnie.
OFTEN — hiyu times.
OIL — glease.
OIL, TO — mamook glease.
OIL CLOTH — snass sail.
OILY — kahkwa glease.
OINTMENT — lametsin; lametsin kopa skin.
OLD MAN — oleman.
OLD WOMAN — lamai.
OMIT — mahsh.
ON — kopa.
ONCE — kopet ikt time.
ONE — ikt.
ONE OR ANOTHER — ikt-ikt.
ONE-EYED — ikt seeowist.
ONION — ulalach.
ONLY — kopet ikt.
OPEN — hahlakl.
OPERATE — mamook.

OPINION — tumtum.
OPPOSITE — enati.
OR — pe.
ORATION — wawa.
ORATOR — man yaka delate kumtux potlatch wawa.
ORDER, TO — mahsh wawa; potlatch wawa.
ORCHARD — kah hiyu apple stick mitlite.
ORE — chikamin stone.
ORIGINAL — chee.
ORNAMENTAL (gay colors) — tzum.
ORPHAN — halo papa halo mama.
OTHER — huloima.
OTTER (sea) — nawamooks.
OTTER (land) — nenamooks.
OUGHT — delate kloshe.
OUR, OURS — nesika; kopa nesika.
OURSELVES — nesika self.
OUT, OUTDOORS, OUTSIDE — klahanie.
OUTLAW — hyas mesachie tillikum.
OVAL — kahkwa egg.
OVEN — oven; kah mamook piah sapolil.
OVER (above) — saghalie.
OVER (other side) — enati.
OVERALLS — klahanie sakoleks.
OVERCOAT — hyas kapo.
OVERBOARD — klahanie kopa boat.
OVERCOME — tolo.
OVERSHOES — klahanie shoes; saghalie shoes.
OVERTHROW — mamook halo; tolo.
OWL — waugh waugh; kwel kwel.
OX — man moosmoos; moosmoos.
OYSTER — chetlo; kloh-kloh.

P

PACIFY — mamook kloshe.
PACK — ikt kow.
PACK, TO — lolo.
PACKAGE — ikt kow.
PADDLE — isick.
PADDLE, TO — mamook isick.
PAID — iskum pay; dolla.
PAIN — sick; pain; addedah; anah.
PAINT — pent.
PAINT, TO — mamook pent.
PAIR — mokst.
PALACE — hyas kloshe house.

PALE — tkope.
PAMPHLET — tenas book.
PAN — ketling.
PANSY — kloshe tupso.
PANT — skookum mamook wind.
PANTHER — hyas pusspuss.
PANTS — sakoleks.
PAPA — papa.
PAPER — pepah.
PAPOOSE — tenas; papoos (seldom used).
PARADE — show.
PARADE, TO — mamook show; kloshe klatawa.
PARDON — mamook klahowya.
PARENTS — papa pe mama.
PARK — kloshe illahee.
PARSON — leplet.
PARSONAGE — leplet yaka house.
PART — sitkum.
PARTAKE — iskum.
PASS, TO — klatawa; klatawa enati.
PASTOR — leplet.
PATERNAL — kahkwa papa.
PATH — ooahut.
PAW — lepee; itswoot yaka lepee (bear, his foot).
PAY — pay; potlatch dolla.
PEAS — lepwah.
PEEP — tenas nanitch.
PELT — skin.
PEN (fence) — kullah.
PEN (for writing) — pen; tzum stick.
PENCIL — pencil; tzum stick.
PENITENT — sick tumtum.
PENITENTIARY — hyas skookum house.
PENMAN — tzum man.
PENTECOST — lapatkot.
PEOPLE — tillikum; tillikums.
PERFECT — delate kloshe.
PERFUME — lametsin kopa nose.
PERHAPS — klonas.
PERIL — mesachie mitlite.
PERMANENT — kwonesum mitlite.
PERMIT — wawa nowitka.
PERPETUAL — kwonesum.
PERSPIRATION — chuck mitlite kopa skin.
PERSPIRE — chuck kopa skin.
PERSEVERE, PERSIST — mamook kwonesum.

PERSON — tillikum.
PERSUADE — wawa pe toto.
PERSON — tillikum.
PERUSE — mamook read.
PETRIFIED — chako stone.
PETTICOAT (or skirt) — kalakwahtee.
PHOTOGRAPH — tzum seeowist.
PHYSIC — lametsin.
PHYSICIAN — doctin.
PICK (select) — ticky.
PICNIC — muckamuck hehe.
PICTURE — tzum pepah.
PIECE — sitkum.
PIETY — kloshe tumtum kopa Saghalie Tyee.
PIG — cosho; tenas cosho.
PIGEON — kwass kalakala.
PILOT — man yaka mamook cooley.
PILL — lametsin.
PIN — kwekweens.
PINE — lagome stick.
PIPE — lapeep.
PITCH — lagome.
PITCHY — lagome mitlite.
PITY, TO — mamook klahowya.
PLACE (his) — kah yaka mitlite.
PLAIN (prairie) — kloshe illahee.
PLAIN — kloshe; delate.
PLAN — tumtum.
PLAN, TO — mamook tumtum.
PLANK — laplash.
PLATE — lasiet.
PLAY — hehe.
PLAY, TO — mamook hehe.
PLAYHOUSE — hehe house.
PLAY WITH STRINGED INSTRUMENT — mamook tuletule.
PLEAD — skookum wawa.
PLEASANT — kloshe.
PLEASED — yotl.
PLENTIFUL — hiyu.
PLOW — lashalloo.
PLOW, TO — mamook kokshut illahee.
PLURAL — hiyu.
POLE — lapehsh.
POND — memaloose chuck.
PONDER — mamook tumtum.
POOL — tenas chuck.

POOR — halo ikta; klahowyum.
POPE — lepapa.
POPULAR — kloshe kopa hiyu tillikums.
POPULATION — tillikums.
PORK — cosho; cosho itlwillie.
POSSESS — mitlite.
POSSIBLE — skookum kopa.
POSTMASTER — tyee kopa pepah house.
POSTPONE — wawa "alki mamook."
POTATO — wappato.
POTENT — skookum.
POUND — pound; till.
POUR — mahsh; wagh.
POVERTY — klahowyum.
POWDER — polallie.
POWER — skookum.
PRACTICE — mamook.
PRAIRIE — kloshe illahee; tupso illahee.
PRAIRIE WOLF — talapus; hyas opoots talapus; literally, big-tail wolf.
PRAISE — wawa mahsie.
PRAY — wawa kopa Saghalie Tyee.
PRAYER — wawa kopa Saghalie Tyee; plie; laplie.
PREACHER — leplet.
PRECIOUS — hyas kloshe; hyas mahkook.
PRECISE — delate.
PREFER — elip ticky.
PREGNANT — mitlite tenas kopa yaka belly.
PREPARE — mamook kloshe.
PRESENT — cultus potlatch.
PRESENTLY — alki; winapee.
PRESERVE — kloshe nanitch.
PRESIDENT — tyee kopa Washington. (Chief at Washington.)
PRESS — mamook kwutl.
PRETEND — halo delate mamook; wawa.
PRETTY — kloshe; toketie.
PREVAIL — tolo.
PRICE (what) — kunsih dolla.
PRICK — mamook kahkwa tupshin.
PROUD — yotl tumtum.
PRIEST — leplet.
PRIME — elip.
PRINT — mamook tzum.
PRIOR — elip.
PRISON — skookum house.
PRISONER — tillikum kopa skookum house.
PRIVATE — kopet ikt.

PROBABLY — klonas.
PROBABLY NOT — klonas halo.
PROCLAIM, PROCLAMATION — wawa.
PROFANE — wake kloshe kopa Saghalie Tyee.
PROFIT — tolo.
PROGENITOR — ahnkuttie papa.
PROHIBIT — mamook stop; mamook kopet.
PROMISE — delate wawa.
PROMPT — hyak.
PROPHET — leplet yaka wawa elip; plopet.
PROSPER — tolo.
PROTECT — kloshe nanitch.
PROUD — yotl; kwelth.
PROVE — delate kumtux.
PROVIDE — iskum iktas; kloshe nanitch.
PROVIDED THAT — spose.
PROVOKE — mamook solleks.
PROVOKED (be) — chako solleks.
PROW — nose kopa boat, ship.
PROWL — cultus klatawa.
PUBLIC — kloshe kopa konaway tillikums.
PUBLISH — mamook kumtux.
PUGILIST — man yaka ticky pight.
PUGNACIOUS — ticky pight.
PUKE — muckamuck yaka killapi; killapi muckamuck; mahsh yaka mucka-
    muck klahanie kopa yaka lapush.
PULL — haul.
PUP, PUPPY — tenas kahmooks.
PURCHASE — mahkook.
PURE — delate kloshe.
PURPLE — wake siah klale.
PURPOSE — tumtum.
PURSE — dolla yaka lesak; lesak kopa dolla.
PURSUE — klatawa kimtah (go after).
PUSH — mamook push; kwutl.
PUT — mahsh.
PUTRID — humm.
PUTRIFY — chako humm.
PUZZLE, TO — halo klap tumtum.

Q

QUAIL — illahee kalakala.
QUAIL, TO — chako kwass.
QUARREL — solleks wawa; tenas pight.
QUARREL, TO — chako solleks; mamook pight.
QUARTER — tenas sitkum.

QUARTER (of a dollar) – kwata.
QUARTERLY – ikt time kopa klone moon.
QUARTZ – tkope stone.
QUEEN – tyee klootchman.
QUEER – huloima.
QUELL, QUENCH – mamook kopet.
QUESTIONS – wawa.
QUICK, QUICKLY – hyak.
QUIET – kwan.
QUILLS – tepeh; kalakala yaka tupso.
QUILT – tzum pasese.
QUIT – kopet.
QUIVER (for arrows) – stick kalitan lesak.
QUORUM – elip sitkum.

R

RABID – hyas solleks.
RABBLE – cultus tillikums.
RABBIT – kwitshadie.
RACE – hyak cooley.
RACE HORSE – cooley kuitan; kuitan yaka kumtux cooley.
RAGGED – iktas yaka kokshut.
RAIN – snass.
RAISE – mamook saghalie.
RAINY – hiyu snass.
RAKE – comb kopa illahee.
RAMBLE – cultus cooley.
RANCH – illahee; ranch.
RAP – mamook kokshut; koko.
RAPE – kapswolla klootchman.
RAPID – hyak.
RAPIDS – skookum chuck; cooley chuck.
RARE – wake hiyu.
RASCAL – mesachie tillikum.
RASP (file) – hyas pile; hyas laleem.
RASPBERRIES – seahpo olallie.
RAT – hyas hoolhool; coleecolee.
RATHER – elip ticky.
RATTLE (shake) – shugh.
RATTLESNAKE – shugh opoots.
RAVE – chako clazy.
RAVEN – kahkah (caw caw).
RAW – wake yaka piah; halo piah.
RAZOR, KNIFE – opitsah.
RAZOR CLAMS – ona.
REACH (to arrive) – ko.

READ, TO — kumtux pepah; kumtux book.
REAL, REALLY — delate.
REAP — mamook cut.
REAR — kimtah.
REASON, TO — mamook tumtum.
REASSEMBLE — weght klatawa.
REASSERT — weght wawa.
REBEL, REBELLION — pight kopa tyee.
REBUILD — weght mamook house.
REBUKE — skookum wawa.
RECALL — weght wawa.
RECEDE — killapi.
RECEIVE — iskum.
RECENT — chee.
RECKON — mamook tumtum.
RECLINE — mitlite.
RECOGNIZE — kumtux.
RECOLLECT — klap tumtum.
RECOMMEND — wawa kloshe.
RECONQUER — weght tolo.
RECONSIDER — weght mamook tumtum.
RECOUNT — weght wawa.
RECOVER — iskum.
RECREATION — kloshe time.
RECUMBENT — mitlite.
RED — pil.
REDDEN — pilpil.
REDDISH — wake siah pil; kahkwa pil.
RED HOT — hyas waum pe chako pil.
REDUCE — mamook keekwullie.
RE-EMBARK — weght klatawa kopa boat.
RE-ENTER — weght klatawa kopa house.
REFINE — mamook delate kloshe.
REFORM — chako kloshe.
REFRESH — chako chee.
REFUND — killapi dolla.
REFUSAL, EXPRESSION OF — kwish.
REFUSE, TO — wawa halo; (if unobligingly) mamook kwish.
REGRET — sick tumtum.
REGULAR — kwonesum kahkwa.
REJECT — mahsh.
REJOICE — yotl tumtum.
RELATE, TO — yiem; wawa.
RELATION, RELATIVE — tillikum.
RELEASE — mahsh, mahsh kow.
RELIABLE — kloshe; halo nika kwass kopa yaka.

RELIEF — help.
RELIEVE — mamook help; potlatch help.
RELIGION — saghalie tyee yaka wawa.
RELISH — kloshe kopa lapush.
REMAIN — mitlite.
REMARRY — weght mallie.
REMEDY — kloshe lametsin.
REMEDY, TO — mamook kloshe.
REMEMBER (not to forget) — mitlite kopa tumtum; wake kopet kumtux.
REMEMBER (to remember after being forgotten) — klip tumtum.
REMIT — mahsh.
REMORSE — sick tumtum.
REMOTE — siah.
REMOUNT — weght klatawa saghalie.
REMOVE — mahsh lolo.
REND — mamook kokshut.
RENEW — mamook chee.
RENOWN — hyas kloshe nem.
REPAIR — mamook kloshe.
REPEAL — mamook halo.
REPEAT — weght wawa.
REPLY — killapi wawa.
REPROVE — potlatch skookum wawa.
RESIDE — mitlite.
RESOLUTE — skookum tumtum.
RESOLVE — mamook tumtum.
REST — cultus mitlite.
RESTAURANT — muckamuck house.
RETREAT, RETURN, REVERSE — killapi.
REVIEW — mamook tumtum.
REVIVE — wind killapi.
RIBBON — leloba.
RIBS — telemin.
RICE — lice.
RICH — halo klahowyum; mitlite hiyu iktas pe dolla.
RID (get rid of) — mahsh.
RIDE — klatawa kopa kuitan or chikchik.
RIDICULE — shem; hehe.
RIDICULE, TO — mamook shem; mamook hehe.
RIFLE — calipeen.
RIGHT (good) — kloshe.
RIGHT (at the) — kenkiam.
RIGHT HAND — kloshe lamah.
RING (for hand) — kweokweo.
RING THE BELL — mamook tintin.
RIPE — piah.

RIPEN — chako piah.
RISE, GET UP — mitwhit.
RISK — cultus kopa nika; (I will risk it) halo nika kwass.
RIVER — chuck; cooley chuck; livah.
ROAD — ooahut; wayhut.
ROAM — klatawa kah.
ROAST — pellah; mamook piah; mamook cook.
ROB — kapswolla.
ROBIN — pil koaten.
ROCK, STONE — stone.
ROCKY — hiyu stone mitlite.
ROE (of fish) — pish eggs; pish lesep.
ROLL — killapi.
ROOT — stick keekwullie kopa illahee.
ROPE — lope.
ROSE — kloshe tupso.
ROSIN — lagome; kull lagome.
ROT — chako lotten.
ROTTEN — poolie; lotten.
ROUND (circular) — tsole.
ROUND (like a sphere) — lowullo.
ROVE — cultus klatawa; cultus cooley.
ROW, TO — mamook lalahm.
ROWER — man yaka kumtux mamook lalahm.
RUBBER COAT — snass coat.
RUDDER — ludda.
RUDE — cultus.
RUIN — mamook halo.
RUM — lum; whiskey.
RUMOR — cultus wawa.
RUN — hyak cooley.
RUN AWAY — kapswolla klatawa.
RUPTURE — kokshut.
RUST — pil ikta kopa chikamin.

S

SABBATH, SUNDAY — Sante.
SABLE — mink.
SACK — lesak.
SACRAMENT — Jesus yaka muckamuck; saklema.
SACRED — kloshe kopa Saghalie Tyee.
SAD — sick tumtum.
SADDLE — lasell.
SADDLE BLANKET — lepishemo.
SAFE — kloshe.

SAIL — sail.
SAILOR — shipman.
SAINT — lesai.
SAINT JOHN — Sai Sha.
SALESMAN — mahkook man.
SALAL BERRIES — salal olallie.
SALMON — sammon.
SALT — salt.
SAME — kahkwa.
SAND — polallie; polallie illahee; tenas stone kahkwa polallie.
SANGUINE — skookum tumtum.
SAP — chuck kopa stick.
SASH — lasanshel; belt.
SATAN — deaub.
SATANIC — kahkwa deaub.
SATISFIED (I am) — kloshe kopa nika.
SATURDAY — taghum sun.
SAVAGE — siwash.
SAVE — iskum.
SAW — lasee.
SAY, TO — wawa.
SCALES — ikta kopa mamook till.
SCANT, SCANTY — wake hiyu.
SCARCE — wake hiyu.
SCARE — mamook kwass.
SCARF — hyas sail kopa neck.
SCATTER — mahsh konaway kah.
SCENT (unpleasant) — humm.
SCENT, TO — mamook humm.
SCHOLAR — tenas kopa school; school tenas.
SCHOONER — mokst stick ship.
SCISSORS — leseezo; sezo.
SCOLD — skookum wawa.
SCREAM — hyas skookum cly.
SCRIPTURE, BIBLE — Saghalie Tyee yaka book; pepah.
SCYTHE — hyas knife kopa hay; yotlkut opitsah.
SEA — salt chuck, sea, wecoma.
SEAL — olhiyu; siwash cosho.
SECOND — mokst.
SECRET — ipsoot.
SECURE — kloshe.
SEDUCE — kapswolla.
SEE, TO — nanitch.
SEEK — mamook hunt; klatawa pe ticky klap.
SEIZE — iskum.
SELDOM — wake hiyu.

SELECT — iskum ikta mika ticky.
SELL, TO — mahsh mahkook.
SEND — mahsh.
SENIOR — elip.
SENSE — kumtux; latate.
SEPARATE (to be) — huloima.
SEPARATE, TO — mamook cut.
SERIOUS — wake hehe.
SERMON — Saghalie Tyee yaka wawa.
SERPENT — oluk; snake.
SERVANT — kahkwa elitee.
SERVE — mamook.
SEVEN — sinamokst.
SEVENTEEN — tahtlum pe sinamokst.
SEVENTY — sinamokst tahtlum.
SEVERAL — tenas hiyu.
SEW, TO — mamook tupshin; mamook sew.
SHACKLE — mamook kow; mahsh chikamin kopa yaka lamah.
SHAKE, TO — toto; hullel.
SHALL — alki; byby; winapee.
SHALLOW — wake keekwullie.
SHAME — shem.
SHAMELESS — halo shem; halo kumtux shem.
SHARE (it is my) — okoke nikas; okoke kopa nika.
SHARK — hyas kahmooks pish.
SHARP — yakkisilth.
SHARPEN, TO — mamook tsish.
SHATTER — mamook kokshut.
SHE, HER — yaka.
SHEEP — lemooto.
SHEET — sail.
SHELL MONEY — coopcoop; allekacheek; hykwa; hiagua.
SHINGLE — lebahdo.
SHINE, TO — mamook kloshe.
SHINING — towagh.
SHIP — ship.
SHIRT — shut.
SHOAL — wake keekwullie.
SHOES — shoes; shush.
SHOOT, TO — mamook poh.
SHORE — illahee.
SHORE (away from) — mahtlinnie.
SHORE (toward) — mahtwillie.
SHORT — yotskut; halo long.
SHORTLY — alki; winapee.
SHOT — tenas lebal; kalitan.

SHOT POUCH — kalitan lesac; tsolepat.
SHOULDERS — okchok.
SHOUT, TO — hyas wawa.
SHOVEL — lapell.
SHOWER — tenas snass.
SHRIEK — skookum wawa.
SHUDDER — kwass pe shake.
SHUT, TO — ikpooie; mamook ikpooie.
SHY — kwass.
SICK — etsitsa.
SICKEN — mamook sick.
SICKLY — tenas sick.
SIDE — (this side) yukwa; (that side) yahwa.
SIFT, TO — toto.
SIGH — tenas cly.
SIGHTLESS — halo nanitch; blind.
SIGN — kahkwa picture.
SILENCE — halo noise.
SILENCE, TO — kopet noise.
SILK — lasway; slik cloth; skookum sail.
SILLY — kahkwa pelton.
SILVER — tkope chikamin; tkope dolla.
SIMILAR — kahkwa.
SIMMER — tenas liplip.
SIN, SINFUL — mesachie.
SINCE — kimtah.
SINCERE — delate.
SING, TO — shantie.
SINGLE — kopet ikt.
SINK, TO — mahsh keekwullie.
SINNER — mesachie tillikum.
SIP — muckamuck chuck.
SIRUP — melass; silup.
SISTER (if older than speaker) — elip ats.
SISTER (if younger than the speaker) — ats.
SISTERLY — kahkwa ats.
SIT, TO — mitlite.
SIX — taghum.
SIXTEEN — tahtlum pe taghum.
SIXTY-ONE — taghum tahtlum pe ikt.
SIZE (what) — kunsih hyas.
SKEPTIC — man yaka halo iskum Saghalie Tyee yaka wawa.
SKILL — kumtux mamook.
SKIN — skin.
SKULL — bone kopa seeowist (point to it).
SKUNK — humm opoots.

SKY — koosah; saghalie.
SLAB — cultus laplash.
SLANDER — mesachie wawa; kliminawhit wawa.
SLAP — mamook kokshut.
SLAVE — elitee; mistchimas.
SLAY — mamook memaloose.
SLEEP — moosum; sleep.
SLEEPLESS — halo moosum; halo sleep.
SLEEPY — ticky moosum; ticky sleep.
SLEIGHT OF HAND — tahmahnawis.
SLIGHT (small) — tenas.
SLING, TO — mahsh.
SLING — tenas lope kopa mahsh stone.
SLIP — wake siah fall down.
SLIPPERY — cultus; loholoh.
SLOW, SLOWLY — klawah; wake hyak.
SLUT — klootchman kahmooks.
SLY — ipsoot.
SMALL — tenas.
SMELL (a) — humm.
SMILE — tenas hehe.
SMITE — mamook kokshut.
SMOKE — smoke.
SMOKE, TO — mamook smoke.
SMOKY (very) — hiyu smoke.
SMOOTH — kloshe.
SNAKE — oluk.
SNARE, TRAP — lepiege.
SNOW — snow, cole snass.
SO — kahkwa.
SOAK — mitlite kopa chuck.
SOAP — soap.
SOFT — klimmin.
SOIL — illahee.
SOLDIER — sogah (army—hiyu sogahs).
SOLELY — kopet.
SOLICIT — wawa; ask.
SOLITARY — kopet ikt.
SOME — tenas hiyu; sitkum.
SOMETIMES — tenas hiyu times.
SOMEBODY — ikt man; klonas klaksta.
SON — tenas.
SOON — alki.
SORCERER — tahmahnawis man.
SORE — sick.
SORRY, SORROW — sick tumtum.

SOUL — tumtum.
SOUND — noise; latlah.
SOUP — lasup; liplip muckamuck.
SOUR — kwates.
SOUTH — kah sun mitlite kopa sitkum sun.
SOW — klootchman cosho.
SOW, TO — mahsh.
SPADE — lapell.
SPARK — tenas piah.
SPARROW — tenas kalakala.
SPEAK, TO — wawa.
SPEAKER — wawa man; man yaka kumtux wawa.
SPECTACLES — glass seeowist; dolla seeowist; lakit seeowist.
SPEED, SPEEDY — hyak.
SPEND — mahsh.
SPIDER — skookum (when spoken of as a tahmahnawis).
SPILL, TO — wagh; mahsh.
SPINE — bone kopa back.
SPIRIT — tumtum; life.
SPIRIT (guardian) — tahmahnawis.
SPIRITS — lum; whiskey.
SPIT — mahsh lapush chuck.
SPIT, TO — toh; mamook toh.
SPLENDID — hyas kloshe.
SPLIT — kokshut; chako kokshut; chako tsugh.
SPLIT, TO — mamook tsugh; mamook kokshut.
SPOIL — spoil; chako spoil.
SPOIL, TO — mamook spoil; mamook mesachie; mamook cultus.
SPOON — spoon.
SPORT — hehe.
SPOTTED — tzum; lekye.
SPRING — tenas waum illahee.
SPRING, TO — sopena.
SPURS — leseeblo.
SPY — nanitch skookum.
SQUALL — skookum wind pe snass.
SQUAW — Siwash klootchman.
SQUEAL — wawa kahkwa cosho.
SQUEEZE — kwutl.
SQUIRREL — kwiskwis.
STAB, TO — klemahun; mamook cut; mamook kokshut kopa knife.
STABLE — kuitan house.
STAG — man mowitch.
STAGE — chikchik.
STAGGER — klatawa kahkwa pahtlum man.
STALE — oleman.

STAMPS (postage) — tzum seeowist.
STAND, TO — mitwhit.
STARE — skookum nanitch.
STARS — tsiltsil; chilchil.
START — klatawa; chee klatawa.
STATE — hyas illahee.
STAY, TO — mitlite.
STEADY (be) — kloshe nanitch.
STEAL, TO — kapswolla.
STEAM — smoke.
STEAMER — piah ship; steamboat.
STEEL — chikamin; piah chikamin.
STEER (animal) — tenas man moosmoos.
STENCH — humm; piupiu.
STERN (rear) — opoots.
STEW — mamook liplip; lakanim.
STICK — stick.
STICK, TO — mamook cut; mamook kwutl.
STILL (be) — kloshe kopet.
STILL (quiet) — kloshe.
STING — opoots klemahun.
STINK (a) — piupiu; humm.
STIR — tenas klatawa.
STIRRUP — sitlay.
STOCKINGS — stocken; kushis.
STOMACH — belly; yakwahtin.
STONE — stone.
STONY — kahkwa stone; stone mitlite.
STOOPED — lagh.
STOP (command) — kopet.
STOP, TO — mamook kopet; ikpooie.
STORE — mahkook house.
STOREKEEPER — mahkook man.
STORM — (wind) hiyu wind; (rain) hiyu snass.
STORY — ekkahnam; wawa; yiem.
STOVE — stob; chikamin piah.
STRAIGHT — delate; delet; sipah.
STRAIGHTEN — mamook delate.
STRANGE — huloima tillikum.
STRAP — skin lope.
STRAP, TO — mamook kow.
STRAWBERRIES — amoteh.
STRAY — cultus klatawa; klatawa kah.
STREAM — chuck; cooley chuck.
STREET — ooahut kopa town.
STRIKE — mamook kokshut.

STRING — tenas lope.
STRIPES — tzum.
STRIVE — mamook skookum.
STROLL — cultus klatawa; cultus cooley.
STRONG — skookum.
STRONGLY — kahkwa skookum.
STUDENT — school tenas; tenas kopa school.
STUDY — mamook tumtum kopa pepah (or book).
STUPENDOUS — delate hyas.
STUPID — halo latate; kahkwa pelton.
STUPOR — kahkwa memaloose.
STURGEON — stutchin.
SUBMERGE — mahsh keekwullie kopa chuck.
SUBMIT — kopet.
SUBSCRIBE — mamook tzum.
SUBSEQUENT — kimtah.
SUBTRACT — mamook haul.
SUCCEED — tolo.
SUCH — kahkwa.
SUCK — muckamuck.
SUDDEN, SUDDENLY — hyak.
SUGAR — shugah; lesook.
SUGARY — kahkwa shugah.
SUICIDE, TO COMMIT — mamook memaloose yaka self.
SUITABLE — kloshe.
SULKY, SULLEN — solleks.
SUM — konaway.
SUMMER — waum illahee.
SUMMON — wawa kloshe yaka chako.
SUN — sun, otelagh.
SUNDAY — Sunday; Sante.
SUNLIGHT — sun yaka light.
SUNRISE — tenas sun; get up sun.
SUNSET — tenas polaklie; klip sun.
SUP, SUPPER — muckamuck kopa tenas polaklie.
SUPPORT — kloshe nanitch; potlatch muckamuck pe konaway iktas.
SUPPOSE — spose.
SUPREME — elip hyas kopa konaway.
SURE — delate; delate kumtux.
SURGEON — doctin.
SURMISE — mamook tumtum; tumtum.
SURPRISE — mamook tumtum; ikta okoke.
SURRENDER — kopet.
SURVEY — mamook tzum illahee.
SURVIVOR — man halo memaloose.
SWALLOW — tenas kalakala.

SWALLOW, TO — muckamuck.
SWAN — kehloke; kahloken; cocumb; ouwucheh; keluk; kaloke.
SWAP — huyhuy.
SWEAR — wawa mesachie; mamook swear.
SWEAT — chuck kopa skin.
SWEEP, TO — mamook bloom.
SWEET — tsee.
SWELL — chako hyas; powil.
SWIFT — hyak.
SWIFT WATER — skookum chuck.
SWIM — sitshum; mamook swim.
SWINE — cosho.
SWING — hang.

T

TABLE — latahb.
TACKS — tenas nails; tenas lekloo.
TAIL — opoots.
TAKE, TO — iskum.
TAKE CARE — kloshe nanitch.
TAKE OFF, OR TAKE OUT — mamook haul; mamook klah; mamook klak; mahsh.
TALE, OR STORY — wawa; yiem; ekkahnam.
TALK — wawa.
TALKATIVE — hiyu wawa.
TALL — hyas tall.
TALLOW — moosmoos glease.
TAMBOURINE OR INDIAN DRUM — pompon.
TAME — halo wind; halo lemolo; kwan.
TAME, TO — mamook kwan.
TAP — tenas kokshut.
TART — tenas sour; tenas kwates.
TASK — mamook.
TASTE — tenas muckamuck.
TATTLE — cultus wawa; yiem.
TAVERN — muckamuck house.
TEA — tea.
TEACH, TO — mamook kumtux; mamook teach.
TEAR — chuck kopa seeowist; kluh.
TEAT — tatoosh.
TEDIOUS — till; long.
TEETH — latah.
TELL, TO — wawa; yiem.
TEMPLE — hyas church house.
TEMPT — haul kopa mesachie.
TEN — tahtlum.

TEND — kloshe nanitch.
TENDER — wake kull; wake skookum.
TENT — sail house.
TERM (of school) — kwata.
TERRIBLE, TERROR — delate hyas mesachie.
TERRITORY — hyas illahee.
TESTICLE — stone.
TESTIMONY — wawa kopa court.
TESTIFY — wawa kopa court; delate yiem.
THAN — kopa.
THANKS, THANKFUL — mahsie.
THAT — okoke.
THAT WAY — yahwa.
THAW — (water) chako chuck; (land) chako klimmin.
THE — sometimes okoke is used—a very definite "the" almost equal to "that."
THEE — mika.
THEFT — kapswolla.
THEIR, THEIRS — klaska.
THEM — klaska.
THEMSELVES — klaska self.
THERE — yahwa; kopa.
THEREABOUT — wake siah yahwa.
THEY — klaska.
THICK (like molasses) — pitlill.
THIEF — kapswolla man; tillikum, yaka kumtux kapswolla.
THIGH — lepee yahwa (pointing to it).
THIN (like paper) — pewhattie.
THINE — mika.
THING — ikta.
THINGS — iktas.
THINK — tumtum; mamook tumtum.
THIRD — klone.
THIRSTY — olo kopa chuck.
THIRTEEN — tahtlum pe klone.
THIRTY — klone tahtlum.
THIRTY-ONE — klone tahtlum pe ikt.
THIS — okoke.
THIS WAY — yukwa.
THITHER — yahwa.
THORN — needle kopa stick.
THOROUGH — delate.
THOSE — okoke.
THOU, THY, THINE — mika.
THOUGHT — tumtum.
THOUGHTLESS — halo tumtum.
THOUSAND — thousand; tahtlum tukamonuk.

THRASH — mamook pat.
THREAD — klapite.
THREAT — mamook kwass.
THREE — klone.
THRONG — hiyu tillikums.
THROW, THRUST, THROW AWAY — mahsh.
THUMB — lamah (pointing to it.)
THUNDER — skookum noise kopa saghalie.
THURSDAY — lakit sun.
THUS — kahkwa.
THYSELF — mika self.
TIDE — chuck chako pe klatawa.
TIE, TO — mamook kow.
TIGER — hyas pusspuss.
TIMBER — stick.
TIME — laly.
TIMID — kwass.
TIN, TINWARE — malah; tin; matah.
TINT — tzum.
TIP, TO — lagh.
TIRE (of a wagon) — chikchik; chikamin.
TIRED — till.
TO, TOWARDS — kopa.
TOBACCO — bacca; kinootl; kinoos; kimoolth.
TODAY — okoke sun.
TOGETHER — kunamokst.
TOMB — memaloose illahee.
TOMORROW — tomolla.
TONGUE — lalang.
TONIGHT — okoke polaklie.
TOO — kunamokst.
TOOTHACHE — sick kopa tooth.
TOP — saghalie.
TORN — kokshut.
TORPID — kahkwa memaloose.
TOSS — mahsh.
TOTAL — konaway.
TOUGH — skookum; kull.
TOW — mamook haul.
TOWARD — kopa.
TOWEL — sail yaka mamook dly; seeowist pe lamah.
TRACK — tzum kah.
TRADE — huyhuy; mahkook.
TRADESMAN — mahkook man.
TRADITION — ahnkuttie tillikums klaska wawa.
TRAIL — ooahut; tenas ooahut.

TRAMP — klatawa kopa lepee.
TRANSFER — lolo.
TRANSGRESSOR — mesachie man.
TRANSLATE — mamook cooley kopa huloima lalang.
TRANSMIT — mahsh; send.
TRAP — lepiege.
TRASH — cultus iktas.
TRAVEL — klatawa; cooley.
TRAVELER — man yaka hiyu cooley.
TREACHEROUS — hyas tseepe; mesachie.
TREASURER — tillikum yaka kloshe nanitch dolla.
TREE — stick.
TREE, FALLEN — whim stick.
TREMBLE, SHAKE — hullel.
TRIBE — lalang.
TRICK — tseepe mamook.
TRIM, TO — mamook cut; mamook kloshe.
TROT, TO — tehteh.
TROUBLE — trouble.
TROUBLE, TO — mamook trouble; mamook till tumtum.
TROUSERS — sakoleks.
TROUT — trout; tenas fish; tzum sammon; tenas sammon.
TRUE — delate; halo kliminawhit.
TRUTH — delate wawa.
TRUNK — lacaset.
TUB — tamolitsh.
TUESDAY—mokst sun.
TURN — killapi; howh.
TURNIP — turnip; lenawo.
TWELVE — tahtlum pe mokst.
TWENTY — mokst tahtlum.
TWENTY-ONE — mokst tahtlum pe ikt.
TWILIGHT — tenas polaklie.
TWINE — tenas lope; klapite.
TWIST — mamook killapi (showing how).
TWO, TWICE — mokst.
TYRO — halo kumtux.

U

UDDER — tatoosh.
UGLY — cultus; wake toketie.
ULTIMATE — kimtah; halo huloima.
UMBRELLA — tenas sail house kopa snass.
UNABLE — wake skookum.
UNACCUSTOMED, UNACQUAINTED — halo kumtux.
UNAWARE — halo kumtux.

UNBELIEF — halo iskum kopa tumtum.
UNBIND — mahsh kow.
UNCEASING — kwonesum.
UNCHRISTIAN — halo kahkwa Jesus.
UNCIVILIZED — wild.
UNCLE — tot; uncle; papa or mama yaka ow; chee.
UNCLEAN — hiyu mesachie mitlite.
UNCONSCIOUS — kahkwa memaloose.
UNCORK — mamook open.
UNDER — keekwullie.
UNDERSTAND — kumtux.
UNDOUBTED — delate.
UNDRESS — mahsh iktas.
UNDYING — halo memaloose.
UNEQUAL — wake kahkwa.
UNEXPECTED (to me) — nika tumtum halo yaka chako kahkwa.
UNEXPLORED — halo klaksta nanitch.
UNFASTEN — mahsh kow.
UNFAVORABLE — halo kloshe.
UNFINISHED — halo kopet.
UNGODLY — mesachie.
UNHAPPY — sick tumtum.
UNINTELLIGIBLE — halo kumtux.
UNIT — ikt.
UNITE — mamook join; mamook kunamokst; chako kunamokst.
UNIVERSAL — konaway.
UNIVERSE — konaway illahee konaway kah.
UNJUST — wake delate.
UNKIND — wake kloshe.
UNKNOWN — halo kumtux.
UNLAWFUL — wake kloshe kopa law.
UNLOAD — mahsh iktas.
UNLOCK — mamook halo lekleh.
UNMEANING — cultus; pelton.
UNNOTICED — halo nanitch.
UNPOPULAR — konaway tillikums halo ticky kahkwa.
UNSALABLE — wake kloshe kopa mahkook.
UNTAMED — lemolo; wild.
UNTIE, TO — mahsh kow; mamook stoh.
UNTO — kopa.
UNTOLD — halo wawa.
UNTRUE — kliminawhit.
UNTURNED — halo killapi.
UNUSUAL — huloima.
UNWILLING — halo ticky.
UNWIND — mamook killapi.

UNWISE — pelton.
UNWHOLESOME — wake kloshe.
UNWORTHY — halo kloshe; wake kloshe; mesachie.
UP — saghalie.
UPBRAID — cultus wawa.
UPHEAVE — mahsh kopa saghalie.
UPHOLD — mamook help; mamook skookum.
UPLAND — saghalie illahee.
UPON — saghalie kopa.
UPPER, UPPERMOST — elip saghalie.
UPRIGHT — delate; kloshe; mitwhit.
UPSET, UPSIDE DOWN — killapi.
UPWARD — saghalie.
URGE — skookum wawa.
URINATE — mahsh chuck.
US — nesika.
USE — mamook use.
USEFUL — kloshe.
USELESS — cultus.
USUAL — kahkwa kwonesum.
UTENSIL — ikta.

V

VACANT — halo.
VACCINATE — mahsh lametsin kopa lamah yaka kloshe kopa smallpox.
VAGABOND — cultus tillikum.
VEIL — sail kopa seeowist.
VAIN — yotl; ploud.
VALIANT — skookum tumtum.
VALISE — tenas lacaset.
VALLEY — kloshe illahee; cooley.
VANISH — chako halo.
VARY — mamook huloima.
VARIED (be) — chako huloima.
VAST — hyas.
VEAL — tenas moosmoos yaka itlwillie.
VEGETABLES — konaway muckamuck chako kopa illahee.
VEHEMENT — skookum.
VEHICLE — chikchik.
VEIN — kah pilpil mitlite (pointing to it).
VENGEANCE — hyas solleks.
VENISON — mowitch itlwillie.
VERILY — delate.
VERMIN — inapoo.
VERY — hyas.
VERY SMALL — hyas tenas.

VESSEL — ship.
VEST — lawest.
VICE — mesachie.
VICINITY — wake siah.
VICTOR — tillikum yaka tolo.
VICTORY — tolo.
VICTUALS — muckamuck.
VIEW — nanitch.
VIGIL — wake moosum.
VILE — mesachie.
VILLAGE — tenas town.
VILLAIN — mesachie tillikum.
VINE — stick; yotlkut tupso; stick kahkwa lope.
VIOLENT — skookum.
VIOLIN — tintin.
VIRGIN — wake kumtux man.
VIRTUOUS — kloshe.
VISION — nanitch.
VISIT — klatawa pe nanitch.
VOICE — wawa.
VOLCANO — piah mountain.
VOMIT, TO — wagh; mahsh muckamuck; muckamuck killapi.
VOTE — mamook vote.
VOYAGE — klatawa kopa boat or ship.

W

WADE — klatawa kopa lepee kopa chuck.
WAG — hehe man.
WAGON — chikchik; tsiktsik.
WAIL — hiyu cly.
WAIT — mitlite winapee.
WAKE — halo sleep; halo moosum.
WAKEN — mamook get up.
WALK — klatawa kopa lepee.
WALL — skookum kullah.
WALTZ — tanse.
WAMPUM (shell money) — hykwa, coopcoop, allekacheek.
WANDER, TO — cultus klatawa; tsolo.
WANT, TO — ticky.
WAR — pight.
WARBLE — sing kahkwa kalakala.
WARM — waum.
WARRIOR — pight tillikum; sogah.
WASH, TO — mamook wash.
WASP — andialh.
WASTE — cultus lost; cultus mahsh.

WATCH — tiktik.
WATCH, TO — kloshe nanitch.
WATCHMAN — man yaka kwonesum kloshe nanitch.
WATER — chuck.
WATERFALL — tumwata.
WATERSPOUT — chuck ooahut.
WAVER — wake skookum.
WAVES — hiyu sea; chuck chako solleks.
WAY — ooahut; wayhut.
WE — nesika.
WEAK — wake skookum; halo skookum.
WEAR — mitlite.
WEARY — till.
WEDDING — mallie.
WEDNESDAY — klone sun.
WEED — cultus tupso.
WEEK — Sunday; week.
WEEP — cly.
WEIGH, TO — mamook till.
WELCOME (to you) — kloshe tumtum mika chako.
WELL — kloshe.
WELL, THEN — abba.
WENT — klatawa.
WEST — kah sun klatawa.
WET — pahtl chuck; chuck mitlite.
WHALE — ekkoli.
WHAT — ikta.
WHEAT — sapolil; lewhet.
WHEEL — chikchik; tsiktsik.
WHEN — kunsih.
WHENCE — kah.
WHERE — kah.
WHET — mamook sharp.
WHICH — klaksta.
WHINE — wawa kahkwa cly.
WHIP — lewhet.
WHISKEY — lum; whiskey.
WHISPER — tenas wawa (showing how); ipsoot wawa.
WHISTLE — mamook wind kopa lapush.
WHITE — tkope.
WHITEN — mamook tkope.
WHITEWASH — mamook pent tkope.
WHO — klaksta.
WHOLE — konaway.
WHOSE — klaksta.
WHY — kahta.

WICKED — mesachie; peshak.
WIDE — klukulh.
WIDOW — klootchman yaka man memaloose.
WIFE — klootchman.
WILD — lemolo.
WILD CAT — hyas pusspuss; siwash pusspuss.
WILD ONION — ulalach.
WILL (the) — tumtum.
WILLOW — eena stick.
WIN, TO — tolo.
WIND — wind.
WIND INSTRUMENT — tuletule.
WINDOW — selokemil.
WINDY — hiyu wind.
WINE — wine.
WING — tepeh.
WINK — mamook seeowist.
WINNOW — mamook toto.
WINTER — cole illahee.
WINTRY — kahkwa cole illahee.
WIPE, TO — mamook dly.
WIRE — chikamin lope.
WISDOM — kumtux.
WISE — kumtux.
WISH, TO — ticky.
WITCH — tahmahnawis.
WITH — kunamokst; kopa.
WITHDRAW — mamook killapi.
WITHOUT (not any) — halo.
WITHOUT (not in) — klahanie.
WOLF — leloo.
WOLF (prairie) — talapus.
WOMAN — klootchman.
WOMANLY — kahkwa klootchman.
WOMAN (old) — lamai.
WOMB — lesak kopa klootchman kah tenas mitlite; belly.
WONDER — mamook tumtum.
WOO — hyas ticky.
WOOD, WOODEN — stick.
WOODPECKER — koko stick.
WOOL — sheep yaka tupso lemooto yakso.
WORD — wawa.
WORK, TO — mamook.
WORLD — konaway okoke illahee.
WORN OUT — oleman; cultus.
WORRY — sick tumtum.

WORSHIP — wawa kopa Saghalie Tyee.
WORSE — elip mesachie; kimtah kloshe.
WORST — elip mesachie kopa konaway.
WORTHLESS — cultus.
WORTHY — kloshe.
WOUND, TO — kwult mamook cut; klemahun.
WRAP — mamook kow.
WRESTLE — mamook pight.
WRETCHED — hyas sick tumtum.
WRIST — lamah yahwa (point to it).
WRITE, TO — mamook tzum; mamook pepah.
WRITING — tzum.
WRITER — tzum man.
WRONG — wake kloshe.

Y

YANKEE — Boston man.
YARD — ikt stick.
YAWN — ticky moosum.
YEAR — ikt cole.
YEARN — hyas ticky.
YELL — hyas skookum wawa.
YELLOW — kawkawak.
YELP — kahmooks wawa.
YES — nowitka; ahha.
YES, INDEED — nowitka.
YESTERDAY — tahlkie sun.
YESTERNIGHT — tahlkie polaklie.
YIELD — kopet.
YONDER — yahwa.
YOU, YOUR (if singular) — mika.
YOU, YOUR (if plural) — mesika.
YOUNG — tenas.
YOUNGER — elip tenas.
YOUNGEST — elip tenas kopa konaway.
YOURSELF — mika self.

APPENDIX

During the past century there have been many Chinook dictionaries compiled and printed, and there have also been many attempts by early travelers, pioneers, and missionaries to gather Chinook Jargon into more or less complete vocabularies. The task of examining these has required painstaking and patient effort on the part of the present writer. Following is a list of reference books, including several articles, which the present compiler used in preparing this dictionary and history:

Allen, A. J., Compiler. *Ten Years in Oregon; travels and adventures of Doctor E. White and lady west of the Rocky Mountains . . . containing also a brief history of the missions and settlement of the country; origin of the Provisional Government; number and customs of the Indians; incidents witnessed in the territory; description of the soil, production and climate of the country.* Ithaca, N. Y., Mack, 1848.

――― *Thrilling adventures, travel, and explorations of Dr. Elijah White, among the Rocky Mountains and in the far West.* New York, Yale, 1859.

Armstrong, A. N. *Oregon; comprising a brief history and full description of the territories of Oregon and Washington, the Indian tribes of the Pacific slope, their manners, etc., interspersed with incidents of travel and adventure.* Chicago, Scott, 1857.

Bancroft, Hubert Howe. *Native Races of the Pacific states of North America.* New York, Bancroft Co., 1882.

Blanchet, Francis Norbert. *A Comprehensive, Explanatory, Correct Pronouncing Dictionary and Jargon Vocabulary; to which is added numerous conversations enabling any person to speak the Chinook jargon.* Portland, Oregon Territory, S. J. McCormick, 1853.

Boas, Franz. *Chinook Jargon Songs.* In *Journal of American Folk Lore*, Vol. 1, 1888.

Bolduc, Jean Baptiste. *Mission de la Colombie.* Quebec, Frechette, 1845.

Buchanan, Charles Milton. *Elementary Lessons in the Chinook Jargon as Used by the Indians of Puget Sound.* Mss., Tulalip, Washington, 1900.

Cook, James. *A Voyage to the Pacific Ocean; undertaken by the command of His Majesty for making discoveries in the Northern Hemisphere.* London, Stockdale, 1784.

Coombs, Samuel F. *Dictionary of the Chinook Jargon; as spoken on Puget Sound and the Northwest, with original Indian names for prominent places and localities with their meanings.* Seattle, Washington, Lowman & Hanford, 1891. It follows Gill very closely in its Chinook-English part and has no English-Chinook part.

Cox, Ross. *Adventures on the Columbia River, including the narrative of a residence of six years on the western side of the Rocky Mountains.* London, Colburn, 1831.

—— *The Columbia River; or, Scenes and adventures during a residence of six years on the western side of the Rocky Mountains.* London, Colburn, 1832.

Demers, Modeste. *Chinook Dictionary, Catechism; prayers and hymns composed in 1838 and 1839; revised, corrected and completed in 1867 by F. N. Blanchet; with modifications and additions by L. N. St. Onge.* Montreal, 1871.

—— *Dictionary of Indian Tongues . . . Tsimpsean, Hydah, and Chinook Jargon.* Victoria, B. C., 1862.

Dunn, John. *History of the Oregon Territory and British North-American Fur Trade; with an account of the habits and customs of the principal native tribes on the northern continent.* London, Edwards, 1846. Contains thirty Chinook Jargon words and expressions.

Durieu, Paul. *Bible History . . . Translated into the Chinook Jargon.* Kamloops, B. C., Benziger, 1893. Four hundred and thirty-one Chinook Jargon words. No English-Chinook part.

Eells, Myron. *Manuscript Dictionary of the Chinook Jargon.* 5 vols. folio, 1893. Following is a note from Eells' Introduction to his dictionary:

"A number of dictionaries have been published in the Chinook Jargon language, and it may seem superfluous to write another; still thus far all of them are small and are based on the language as it was forty or fifty years ago. Gibbs' Dictionary was for many years by far the best, and is yet in many respects, as it gives the origin of nearly all the words and much other valuable information, but it was written nearly forty years ago. I have used it very much in preparing this work. Hale's Trade Language of Oregon or Chinook Jargon is recent and is excellent, especially in its Introductory part; far better than any which preceded it, but that excellent man and scholar has labored under the disadvantage of not having mingled much with those who have used the language for about fifty years, and so has been unable to note a great share of the changes which have taken place. The dictionaries of Gill, Hibben, Tate, Lowman and Hanford and Good are all small; are in as condensed form as possible, being intended for pocket use for travellers, traders and learners, and in this way have done good work for what they were intended. The two latter, however, only have the Chinook English part. The dictionary of Durieu is very meager, while that of Demers and St. Onge is out of print, and both are intended rather more for use by the Catholics than by the public. . . .

"Having used it (Jargon) for eighteen years, having talked in it, sung in it, prayed and preached in it, translated considerable into it, and thought in it, I thought I knew a little about the language, but when I began to write this dictionary I found that there was very much which I did not know about it, but which I wished to know in order to make this dictionary as perfect as it should be. . . ."

—— *History of Indian Missions on the Pacific Coast; Oregon, Washington, and Idaho.* Philadelphia, American Sunday-School Union, circa 1882.

—— *Hymns in the Chinook Jargon Language.* Portland, Oregon, Himes, 1881.

—— *Ten Years of Missionary Work among the Indians at Skokomish, Washington Territory.* Boston, Congregational Sunday-School, circa 1886.

Gibbs, George. *A Dictionary of the Chinook Jargon, or, Trade Language of Oregon.* New York, Cramoisy, 1863. This was by far the best dictionary at that time and will ever remain a standard authority on the language of that time. In the Chinook-English part are 490 words, and in the English-Chinook, 792.

Gill, John K. *Gill's Dictionary of the Chinook Jargon.* Portland, Oregon, 1882. In the Chinook-English part are 560 words, and in the English-Chinook, 1,378.

Good, John Booth. *A Vocabulary and Outlines of Grammar of the Nitlakapamuk or Thompson Tongue (the Indian language spoken between Yale, Lillooet, Cache Creek and Nicola Lake); together with a phonetic Chinook dictionary adapted for use in the province of British Columbia.* Victoria, B. C., St. Paul's Mission Press, 1880. It has no Chinook-English part. In the English-Chinook he gives 825 words.

Hale, Horatio E. *An International Idiom; a Manual of the Oregon Trade Language, or Chinook Jargon.* London, Whittaker, 1890. Four hundred and seventy-three Chinook Jargon words; 634 in the English-Chinook part.

Hazlitt, William C. *British Columbia and Vancouver Island; compris-*

ing a historical sketch of the British settlements in the Northwest coast of America. London, Routledge, 1858.

Jewitt, John Rodgers. *A Narrative of the Adventures and Sufferings of John R. Jewitt, Only Survivor of the Crew of the Ship Boston; during a captivity of nearly three years among the savages of Nootka Sound, with an account of the manners, mode of living, and religious opinions of the natives.* (Written by Richard Alsop). Middleton, Conn., Loomis & Richards, 1815.

Lee, Daniel, and Frost, J. H. *Ten Years in Oregon.* New York, Collord, 1844.

LeJeune, John M. *Chinook and Shorthand Rudiments, with which the Chinook Jargon and the Wawa Shorthand can be mastered without a teacher in a few hours, by the editor of the "Kamloops Wawa."* Kamloops, B. C., 1898.

—— *Chinook Primer.* Kamloops, B. C., St. Louis Mission, 1892.

—— *Practical Chinook Jargon Vocabulary.* Kamloops, B. C., St. Louis Mission, 1886.

Macdonald, Duncan G. *British Columbia and Vancouver's Island, Comprising a Description of These Dependencies; also an account of the manners and customs of the native Indians.* London, Longman, 1862.

Macfie, Matthew. *Vancouver Island and British Columbia; their history, resources and prospects.* London, Longman, 1865.

Norris, Philetus W. *The Calumet of the Coteau and Other Poetical legends of the Border; also a glossary of Indian names, words and western provincialisms.* Philadelphia, Lippincott, 1883.

Palmer, Joel. *Journal of Travels over the Rocky Mountains to the Mouth of the Columbia River, 1845 and 1846 . . . including about 300 words of the Chinook Jargon.* Cincinnati, James, 1847.

Parker, Samuel. *Journal of an Exploring Tour beyond the Rocky Mountains; under the direction of the American Board of Commissioners for Foreign Missions, in the years 1835, 1836, and 1837; containing a description of the geography, geology, climate, productions of the country, and the number, manners, and customs of the natives.* Ithaca, New York, 1838.

Phillips, Walter S. *Totem Tales; Indian stories Indians told, gathered in the Pacific Northwest, with a glossary of words, customs and history of the Indians.* Chicago, Star, circa 1896.

Pilling, James C. *Bibliography of the Chinookan Languages, Including the Chinook Jargon.* Washington, D. C., 1893.

—— *Bibliography of the Wakashan Languages.* Washington, D. C., 1893.

Ross, Alexander. *Adventures of the First Settlers on the Oregon or Columbia River; being a narrative of the expedition fitted out by John Jacob Astor to establish the "Pacific Fur Company"; with an account of some Indian tribes on the coast of the Pacific, by one of the adventurers.* London, Smith & Elder, 1849.

Ross gives a "Chinook Vocabulary" and words of the "mixed dialect." His Chinook, however, is impure.

Schoolcraft, Henry R. *Indian Tribes of the United States.* Philadelphia, 1851.

Scouler, John. *"Observations on the Indigenous Tribes of the Northwest Coast of America."* Journal of the Royal Geographical Society of London, Vol. 11, London, 1841.

—— *"On the Indian Tribes Inhabiting the Northwest Coast of America."* New Philosophical Journal, Vol. 41. Edinburgh, 1846.

Shaw, George. *The Chinook Jargon and How to Use It; a complete and exhaustive lexicon of the oldest trade language of the American continent.* Seattle, Rainier Printing Co., 1909.

—— *240 Chinook Jargon Words Used by the Siwash on Puget Sound and by Indians and whites of the great Pacific Northwest for nearly 150 years.* Edited by Nika Tikegh Chikamin (George Coombs Shaw). Seattle, Johnson, 1932.

Sproat, Gilbert M. *Scenes and Studies of Savage Life.* London, Smith & Elder, 1868.

Swan, James G. *The Northwest Coast; or, Three Years' Residence in Washington Territory.* London, Sampson Low, 1857.

In the appendix is a rather full vocabulary—327 words. Judge Swan lived on Shoalwater Bay, Washington, near the Chehalis and Chinook Indians, and he includes a number of words which are given by no other writer, which he says are of Chehalis origin.

Tate, Charles M. *Chinook as Spoken by the Indians of Washington Territory, British Columbia, and Alaska; for the use of traders, tourists and others who have business intercourse with the Indians. Chinook-English, English-Chinook.* Victoria, B. C., Waitt, 1889.

Winthrop, Theodore. *The Canoe and the Saddle; adventures among the northwestern rivers and forests, and Isthmiana.* Boston, Ticknor, 1863. Two hundred and sixty-one Chinook words. There is no English-Chinook part.